Dark Forces

By Paul Karl Hoiland

INTRODUCTION

The story I am about to unfold has all the makings of one of those Hollywood horror block busters that where often in vogue during the later part of the 70's and early 80's complete with the evil and the good each in their respective parts. But this is not fiction, nor will you be seeing it on pay per view. You are witnessing it unfold in the most current events in modern American history from the play out of what has now become known as the Arab Spring, to the subtle unfolding of political campaigns, to the Housing crisis itself. It is the story of the Dark Forces as I have come to call them working in the background behind the everyday News events to some of the more outright moves that so little of the general population has bothered to notice.

It is the story of the take over of the American Dream by what in another era and time would best be described by the more ancient word, ILLUMINATI. Oh, not the scientists of ancient Old World tales that sought at one time to shed light upon the darkness of mental enslavement within the Catholic Church. No, this Illuminati are far more sinister and far less benign. And no, contrary to much of the far right thinking that this is a tale of Socialists and Marxists trying to take over society here and across the world in what they term the Left, this treat to our vary fabric is far worse than anything even Stalin could have imagined. Indeed, it has used both the Left and the Right as Pawns in its game of world domination and at the same time utilized the Church and its social networks to achieve its ends many times with those within it's ranks taking part in this plot with themselves paying little notice to the damage they have caused all the while thinking the laws they have put into place are there to protect our American Way.

To be sure we have been warned by many of our past leaders in this country of this, we have been told many times over in both veiled and clear words of what to look out for. In fact, the warnings go all the way back to the Founding Father's of our Nation, and flow across American History from both President's of our great Nation, and many other members of past Congress', Military Members, honest concerned citizens that saw a rising danger appearing in everything from Politics, to Wall Street, to the Military, to Big Corporations and the multinational Banks that held their purse strings. But it is a warning that most American's have ignored and in some cases helped to foster through both inattention and idealism gone untamed and feral like some stray cat. In other cases, many out there have become the sheep by product of our current dummied down Educational system that has nearly eliminated any honest teaching of the Constitution and honest American History. The end result is the same: A ripe field of crop for the picking and plunder of these Dark Forces at work in the World today.

THE WARNINGS: A Brief history of such

One could best start with the very wording and meaning of our Constitution and even the Declaration of Independence itself. No, our Founding Father's where not prophets like those of ancient Biblical tales. They where student's of history having taken part in a bloody period of world history and had managed to sit back an learn from that history and set forth documents of what could best be described as a New World Order, NOVUS ORDO SECLORUM, as it is termed on our dollar bill, to avoid the mistakes of that past. As such, they where actually just forth telling how to avoid the mistakes of the past, not with a perfect system. But with a more fair system.

The Constitution starts with the words, "WE THE PEOPLE". These are profound words having come from a people who had mostly grown up under the absolute rule of the King of England. To those under the Crown at that time there was no We the People. There was only the King's will. The King held all the power, all the military power, all the economy. In short, the King was absolute ruler of everyday life even down to being head of the Church of England. In short, he ruled every aspect of human existence and collected taxes from everything consumed.   If one dared to question the King in any area of everyday life one was termed an enemy of the State. Persecution for idealism that differed from that of the King was the hallmark of the day. And yet, here we have a rag tag group of colonists under the rule of that King daring to utter the words We the People.

Basically, those famous opening lines where words with an implication nearly the same as those recorded in the Old Testament of the King of Tyre when he started he would place his will above that of God. For indeed, the King of England as head of the Church of England was to many God's representative on earth when it came to the affairs of man. They where in those three great words announcing to the World that the will of the people was to transcend the will of the King.

That great document goes on to speak of the stage of human history and in short summery describes what had led up to this declaration. Without a long story that goes to the heart of the problem they faced, they in short declared that because of this the King was not worthy of absolute authority and that in one voice that the will of the people would now take what once was the authority of the King. What follows then in the Constitution is an outlay of a form of Government that would respect the will of the people, instead of the will of some King.

The Constitution of the United States

We the People of the United States, in Order to form a more perfect Union, establish Justice, insure domestic Tranquility, provide for the common defense, promote the general Welfare, and secure the Blessings of Liberty to ourselves and our Posterity, do ordain and establish this Constitution for the United States of America.

In these opening lines the Constitution spells out the very place and job of our Government which is all People centered. Establish Justice, insure domestic tranquility, provide for the common defense, promote general Welfare, secure Liberty for us and those who come after us. Basically, the idealism they laid out in this long debated and compromised over document gave the Government the job of justice or the rule of law, to maintain domestic tranquility of order, promote the welfare of it's citizens and keeping the Liberties of the People alive.

One of the first things addressed is the issue of funding for the Government to do it's spelled out job.

The Congress shall have Power To lay and collect Taxes, Duties, Imposts and Excises, to pay the Debts and provide for the common Defense and general Welfare of the United States; but all Duties, Imposts and Excises shall be uniform throughout the United States;

This was in answer to what they had faced under the King of England. They sought a fair tax system that was uniform throughout the United States. Anyone who ever tells you that tax collection is unconstitutional has never read the document for themselves. What could be well argued is not Constitutional about our current tax system is that it does not respect that uniformity aspect the Founding Father's intended. We have at present a tax system that does in many ways favor the rich, caters not to companies that promote domestic good, but more serves those who would send the benefit of the labor and production overseas which violates the whole spirit of general Welfare for the citizens of this country. This in itself, a modern outcome of the Dark Forces at work was itself already in the Constitution warned about.

If one counts in all the crazy Environmental Protection Agency laws, which through fine, most paid to our Government, we encounter another rather unequal and unfair taxation of business.

"All Bills for raising Revenue shall originate in the House of Representatives; but the Senate may propose or concur with Amendments as on other Bills."

One can see in this clause that the duty of making sure that tax collection falls within the guidelines of the Constitution lies with the House of Representatives, with the agreement of the Senate and in some cases their own proposal on such. If we have a failure in the area of taxes then that failure lies square upon every member of this branch of our Government more than any other as outlined in the Constitution which is interesting given that our current House is numbered high by GOP members who along Conservative lines claim to stand behind our Constitution, yet, fail in achieving it's goal for that branch.

The Constitution goes on to say:

To borrow Money on the credit of the United States;
To regulate Commerce with foreign Nations, and among the several States, and with the Indian Tribes;
To establish an uniform Rule of Naturalization, and uniform Laws on the subject of Bankruptcies throughout the United States;
To coin Money, regulate the Value thereof, and of foreign Coin, and fix the Standard of Weights and Measures;
To provide for the Punishment of counterfeiting the Securities and current Coin of the United States;
To establish Post Offices and post Roads;
To promote the Progress of Science and useful Arts, by securing for limited Times to Authors and Inventors the exclusive Right to their respective Writings and Discoveries;
To constitute Tribunals inferior to the supreme Court;
To define and punish Piracies and Felonies committed on the high Seas, and Offences against the Law of Nations;
To declare War, grant Letters of Marque and Reprisal, and make Rules concerning Captures on Land and Water;

To raise and support Armies, but no Appropriation of Money to that Use shall be for a longer Term than two Years;
To provide and maintain a Navy;
To make Rules for the Government and Regulation of the land and naval Forces;
To provide for calling forth the Militia to execute the Laws of the Union, suppress Insurrections and repel Invasions;
To provide for organizing, arming, and disciplining, the Militia, and for governing such Part of them as may be employed in the Service of the United States, reserving to the States respectively, the Appointment of the Officers, and the Authority of training the Militia according to the discipline prescribed by Congress;

Before I go on with the rest I would point out several key issues raised by this outline of the duties of Congress.

To declare War, grant Letters of Marque and Reprisal, and make Rules concerning Captures on Land and Water;
To raise and support Armies, but no Appropriation of Money to that Use shall be for a longer Term than two Years;

Here the ability to actual declare war is that of Congress and not the President of the United States. The Founding Father's never intended for one person to decide when and why we as a Nation will go to war. Notice, none of the money specially collected to conduct a war was to be for a period longer than two years. One can also notice the intent of this document that all wars aged would be funded by their own special means up to and including additional taxes. This was true with most of the wars America has fought up until Bush Junior and followed on by the Obama Administration. One will notice however that the training of the Military, selection of Officers, etc was the power of the States and not the Federal Government which runs in the face of our current military going way back to the Civil War times.

One can also note that our current Government and most of the past Administrations has failed totally along the lines of establishing a uniform Rule of Naturalization. Part of this failure stems from both Parties in this Country seeing the vast illegal immigration population as potential votes for their party. So the failure in this case stems from a desire for votes that translates into political power even though they stand in direct violation of the Constitution.

This document goes on to say:

The Privilege of the Writ of Habeas Corpus shall not be suspended, unless when in Cases of Rebellion or Invasion the public Safety may require it.
No Bill of Attainder or ex post facto Law shall be passed.
No Capitation, or other direct, Tax shall be laid, <u>unless in Proportion to the Census or enumeration herein before directed to be taken</u>.

No Tax or Duty shall be laid on Articles exported from any State.

No Preference shall be given by any Regulation of Commerce or Revenue to the Ports of one State over those of another; nor shall Vessels bound to, or from, one State, be obliged to enter, clear, or pay Duties in another.

No Money shall be drawn from the Treasury, but in Consequence of Appropriations made by Law; and a regular Statement and Account of the Receipts and Expenditures of all public Money shall be published from time to time.

Some of the most questionable laws enacted since 911 stem back to the whole Cases of Rebellion. Even though at present the threat is more from the outside this clause has been used to justify laws on our books that violate several key parts of both the Constitution and the Bill of Rights. Politics and World Affairs can make for some very strange Bed Fellows. Such is the case with how many Evangelicals have supported these unconstitutional laws and how many more radical groups like the KKK have supported them. Given the recent Government attempts at limiting Freedom of Religion and how many of the White Supremacy Groups are considered Terrorists themselves their support of these laws may well prove to be the worst tool against them the Government has ever had.

One could argue how well the current Federal Reserve actually follows the letter and spirit of that last part.

No Title of Nobility shall be granted by the United States: And no Person holding any Office of Profit or Trust under them, shall, without the Consent of the Congress, accept of any present, Emolument, Office, or Title, of any kind whatever, from any King, Prince, or foreign State.

There is at present a growing line of argument against the whole Czar title certain members of our Federal Government have been termed, especially since this title is one applied by the President and not Congress.

The executive Power shall be vested in a President of the United States of America. He shall hold his Office during the Term of four Years, and, together with the Vice President, chosen for the same Term, be elected, as follows:

The President shall be Commander in Chief of the Army and Navy of the United States, and of the Militia of the several States, when called into the actual Service of the United States; he may require the Opinion, in writing, of the principal Officer in each of the executive Departments, upon any Subject relating to the Duties of their respective Offices, and he shall have Power to grant Reprieves and Pardons for Offences against the United States, except in Cases of Impeachment.

He shall have Power, by and with the Advice and Consent of the Senate, to make Treaties, provided two thirds of the Senators present concur; and he shall nominate, and by and with the Advice and Consent of the Senate, shall appoint Ambassadors, other public Ministers and Consuls, Judges of the supreme Court, and all other Officers of the United

States, whose Appointments are not herein otherwise provided for, and which shall be established by Law: but the Congress may by Law vest the Appointment of such inferior Officers, as they think proper, in the President alone, in the Courts of Law, or in the Heads of Departments.

The President shall have Power to fill up all Vacancies that may happen during the Recess of the Senate, by granting Commissions which shall expire at the End of their next Session.

Here the Founding Fathers spelled out the powers of the President and the reach of such powers.

The judicial Power of the United States shall be vested in one supreme Court, and in such inferior Courts as the Congress may from time to time ordain and establish. The Judges, both of the supreme and inferior Courts, shall hold their Offices during good Behavior, and shall, at stated Times, receive for their Services a Compensation, which shall not be diminished during their Continuance in Office.

Section. 2.

The judicial Power shall extend to all Cases, in Law and Equity, arising under this Constitution, the Laws of the United States, and Treaties made, or which shall be made, under their Authority;--to all Cases affecting Ambassadors, other public Ministers and Consuls;--to all Cases of admiralty and maritime Jurisdiction;--to Controversies to which the United States shall be a Party;--to Controversies between two or more States;-- between a State and Citizens of another State,--between Citizens of different States,-- between Citizens of the same State claiming Lands under Grants of different States, and between a State, or the Citizens thereof, and foreign States, Citizens or Subjects.

Here they addressed the Court system of this country and the powers of such a system.

The next great document of our Nation is the Bill of Rights. In this document the rights of the People, which where seen by the Founding Fathers as something we as human beings have by virtue of birth, not Government granting of such.

Bill of Rights

Amendment I

Congress shall make no law respecting an establishment of religion, or prohibiting the free exercise thereof; or abridging the freedom of speech, or of the press; or the right of the people peaceably to assemble, and to petition the Government for a redress of grievances.

There are several key rights spelled out in this first Amendment. The first is freedom of Religion. Basically, what is protected here is the right of worshiping God as one personally sees fit without the Government telling one what to believe or not. One notices that the Government cannot prevent the free exercise of that religious choice. In modern times we have had a few unique aspects of this surface. One is the issue about those that are Atheist being forced to attend anything religious in Nature. While it may to many seem contrary for someone who claims no religion or belief in God to seek equality under a law of right that provides for free worship in general it can be well argued that they do have the right to not worship or have religious idealism forced down their throats.

The second aspect of this basic right that has come under review in the area of Government proposed ideas on healthcare is actually the more fundamental arena of battle. Basically, by a strict reading the Constitution does prevent the Government from being able to dictate to the Church's that they have to supply certain healthcare items if those items violate the beliefs of those with a certain Church organization. However, on the reverse side there is nothing, even those beliefs that prevents the Government from doing so themselves even with tax money simply because part of the Government's job is to provide for the common welfare of its people. At this point the Government can act, even with those tax dollars that might have been collected from many within that religious organization that had beliefs against such.

Free Speech is itself seen as a basic right. On the grounds of free speech alone the Government, in more modern terms, does not have the right to declare someone an enemy of this country simply because they think the Government is wrong on an issue. The People have the right to speak out. Now, that does not stop the Government from watching such a person. Nor does it prevent the Government from acting against such a person if that person goes beyond free speech and begins to organize Para-military action against the Government. There are laws in this country that allow the Government to act in such cases. But in no way can and should the Government be allowed to in act laws that in any way hinder the basic right of free speech. Yet, in many ways they already have done such.

A well regulated Militia, being necessary to the security of a free State, the right of the people to keep and bear Arms, shall not be infringed.

This amendment has been argued back and forth on everything except what it was intended for. Basically, the right to bear arms is in our Bill of Rights to allow the people to have the power to protect themselves from tyranny. It is not actually the greatest right we have and in fact, is the last ditch right one can use to prevent say a Government that wants to take away our rights, or an individual that wants to deprive you of your rights in one form or another. But it is a basic right of the people for self protection.

The right of the people to be secure in their persons, houses, papers, and effects, against unreasonable searches and seizures, shall not be violated, and no Warrants shall issue, but upon probable cause, supported by Oath or affirmation, and particularly describing the place to be searched, and the persons or things to be seized.

There are two basic modern rulings or laws of Congress that have totally violated the spirit and the intent of this basic Constitutional Right. One is the so called Patriot Act and the other is the more recent Military Appropriations Bill. The first basically, though the Government claims it has never been used that way allows our Government to spy on its citizens without a search warrant. The second gives the ability to arrest without trial and detain any citizen deemed a terrorists. It also stipulates the Military and not a civilian court would have the ability to try them. Both of these laws while based upon good intentions and a desire to protect our country and it's citizens violates the Constitution and the Bill of Rights and as such are not lawful.

Amendment V
No person shall be held to answer for a capital, or otherwise infamous crime, unless on a presentment or indictment of a Grand Jury, except in cases arising in the land or naval forces, or in the Militia, when in actual service in time of War or public danger; nor shall any person be subject for the same offence to be twice put in jeopardy of life or limb; nor shall be compelled in any criminal case to be a witness against himself, nor be deprived of life, liberty, or property, without due process of law; nor shall private property be taken for public use, without just compensation.

Here again the above two laws stand in opposition to our Bill of Rights.

Amendment VI
In all criminal prosecutions, the accused shall enjoy the right to a speedy and public trial, by an impartial jury of the State and district wherein the crime shall have been committed, which district shall have been previously ascertained by law, and to be informed of the nature and cause of the accusation; to be confronted with the witnesses against him; to have compulsory process for obtaining witnesses in his favor, and to have the Assistance of Counsel for his defense.

This is probably the worst violation built into the MADD Bill. By consigning citizens to a Military Court instead of a civilian one they violate our right to a speedy trial and to judgment by our Peers. This new assault on our Constitution also violates the idea of not being deprived of life, liberty, or property, without due process of law. At least the type of due process intended by our Founding Fathers. The worst thing about all this was only 30 members of Congress voted against this Bill which leaves the blood trail of a major violation of our Constitution on the shoulders of Members of the GOP and the Democratic Party. It is also interesting to note those members of the GOP known as the Tea Party, which ran on a platform of taking back America in many cases voted for that Bill which actually does anything but take back America and makes them guilty of increasing Government intrusion into our lives instead of decreasing it.

Amendment X
The powers not delegated to the United States by the Constitution, nor prohibited by it to the States, are reserved to the States respectively, or to the people.

This is perhaps one of the greatest arguments going in society today between the Federal Government and the States as well as the People. There has in modern times been an attempt on the part of the Left and the Right to increase the power of Government at a Federal level in our lives. While it is true that the Conservatives give lip service to smaller Government they also due to the influence of the so called Religious Right to interject themselves into the area of personal choice and have even voiced idealism to do away with public education and basically force everyone to attend religious run schools which itself violates the spirit of separation of Church and State.

The Left on the other hand has attempted at all avenues to increase its own network of what it provides under the idea of common good in the way of expanded social programs. Neither of these extremes really fulfills the spirit of the Constitution, nor can such be sustained at an ever increasing level without serious budget problems at the moment.

AMENDMENT XIV
Passed by Congress June 13, 1866. Ratified July 9, 1868.
Note: Article I, section 2, of the Constitution was modified by section 2 of the 14th amendment.
Section 1.
All persons born or naturalized in the United States, and subject to the jurisdiction thereof, are citizens of the United States and of the State wherein they reside. No State shall make or enforce any law which shall abridge the privileges or immunities of citizens of the United States; nor shall any State deprive any person of life, liberty, or property, without due process of law; nor deny to any person within its jurisdiction the equal protection of the laws.

This has become a major debate point when it comes to immigration. It is also the fundamental backdrop upon which our Government's refusal to act rests. Basically, many of the illegal immigrants in this country today have children natural born in this country which makes those children citizens by birth. So a very fine line issues forth when it comes to deportation of their illegal Parents since in most cases the Parents would be forced to remove a child who is a citizen from this Country. It also lies at the heart of many of the cases where illegal's end up getting the benefit of our tax dollars even though they generally do not pay anything into the system at all.

Section 4.
The validity of the public debt of the United States, authorized by law, including debts incurred for payment of pensions and bounties for services in suppressing insurrection or rebellion, shall not be questioned. But neither the United States nor any State shall assume or pay any debt or obligation incurred in aid of insurrection or rebellion against the United States, or any claim for the loss or emancipation of any slave; but all such debts, obligations and claims shall be held illegal and void.

It is interesting in a time when neither part of Congress has managed to actually pass a budget that they are in violation of their basic duties at this point, and yet still manage to hold office. One could well argue that Bush Junior violated this when he engaged in a War on two fronts with no actual provision to have that war paid for. One could well argue that the Bail Outs whither good or not violated the spirit of this by taking on more debit than can possible be paid by this country at this time with no plan in mind on how to make sure those debits where meet. While there are many good reasons for America to act when it comes to the turmoil in the Middle East, one could also argue that in many ways our Country's Leaders are creating debit helping those in many cases like the Arab Brotherhood in Egypt and elsewhere who are in direct rebellion against our Country in the first place. Part of the reason this has happened is we simply do not have any solid goal, outside of promoting democracy in that region. The problem is that real Democracy involves people deciding upon their own Government which in many cases might not be prone to working with America at all. So in essence there is serious room to question the spending of our tax dollars in areas that themselves violate our Constitution via aid to those in rebellion against us and our Allies. "But neither the United States nor any State shall assume or pay any debt or obligation incurred in aid of insurrection or rebellion against the United States." Now that does leave open our ability to try and establish treaties with these groups to promote an end to that rebellion. But, in most cases we have simply provided aid and Military support in some cases with little of that last being utilized which makes those debit's a serious violation of the Law of this Country.

I have laid forth these points out of the Constitution and the Bill of Rights as a background to those Dark Forces at work in our Country to compare how this country is supposed to operate in view of how it is operating and to expose just exactly what these Dark Forces are after when it comes to America.

LIBERALISM VERSUS CONSERVATISM

In defining the differences between liberalism and conservatism, there are five main political spectrums to consider. These are:

1. Individualism vs. Altruism
2. Anarchy vs. Organization
3. Democracy vs. Constitutionalism
4. Equality vs. Merit
5. Competition vs. Cooperation

An individualist is someone who is 100 percent self-interested. An altruist is someone who is 100 percent interested in the well-being of others. Of course, there is a spectrum between these two positions.

There are many ways to believe in pure individualism and still allow that individuals can cooperate in the sort of interdependent, specialized society that makes us all richer. Libertarians and extreme conservatives believe in the "invisible hand," a term coined by 18th century economist Adam Smith. In his desire to get rich, a baker bakes bread for hundreds of people, and in this he is led by an "invisible hand" to feed society, even though such altruistic notions were not part of his original intention. When individuals are allowed to seek their own rewards, the argument goes, the common interest naturally takes care of itself. No central authority needs to consciously promote the common interest.

The problem with Libertarian idealism and extreme conservatives is that their ideals work better in a society built around farming more than the society we live in today. They also depend upon the giving hearts of others to support those who cannot work which would be the case in an ideal society with perfect loving people. But most humans have a strong self interest at play that tends to leave a large gap in the supply of the needs of others who cannot work to support themselves.

Anarchy is the ultimate in individual freedom where people can do anything they want. It tends to be a system with little law even though the Freedom of the Individual is upheld. A common philosophy of moderation is: government should support and promote those forms of individual freedom and self-interest which advance the common interest, and prevent those forms of individual freedom and self-interest which harm it.   This is basically the heart and soul of the current major debates over both Gay Marriage and Abortion. The question in the first is not so much about sexual life style as about do they have a right to the same institutional protection heterosexual couples do. The center of the debate on the other issue concerns life and when it starts since the laws of our country are designed to protect living innocence. Most on the one side of the first have moral problems with Gay life style to begin with and believe marriage should be only for one man and one women. The Gay community sees the ban on Gay Marriage as hampering their rights as Americans.

A strict reading of our Constitution does actually give them ground in what they are saying. While being Gay was not a major social issue at the time the Constitution was written, the very words, "WE THE PEOPLE" and the fact that the rights of citizens of this Country are seen as God given or rather, rights one has by virtue of birth tends to argue that they should have the same rights as any other American irrespective of religious views on such given that it is not the place of Government to endorse or enforce those views. So generally, the Conservative thing to do would be to support their rights under the Constitution.

Those who want to ban abortion see it as murder supported by their tax dollars. Those on the other side see it as protection and support of the rights of women over their own bodies and are rather split on the issue of when life actually starts.

Liberals believe that government can actively promote, not just allow, the free market. For example, the government can build roads, wire the countryside for electricity and phone service, launch communication satellites and provide economic statistics, all of which allow the free market to flourish. And liberals believe that the government should be more active in preventing harmful self-interest. For example, they believe government should regulate corporate polluters. Conservatives oppose this, but it is inconsistent with the very philosophy that generates their position on crime since by a lot of laws in this country Pollution is defined as a crime. I would also point out that lack of Pollution control tends to run contrary to the promotion of the well being of all Americans.

The Founding Fathers knew that democracy only works if the voters are educated. The problem back in the 18th century was the majority of Americans were illiterate. The problem today is not so much a lack of education but more the depth of education. More time in school is spent on reading, writing, etc than on either government, history, or economics. Most people have not ever even studied the different systems of government for themselves. They just accept what others like talk show hosts or the News media tells them. We have become a Nation of educated Sheep when it comes to government. We are not much better than the mindless people who join cults and fall prey to what their leaders tell them. The same applies in the average Church today where few ever bother to research something out for themselves. Both could use a direct application of a certain Bible verse that says "Study to show yourself approved…"

Our Founding Fathers designed our government system the best they could to take this into account by creating a representative democracy, or a republic, in which laws were voted upon not by the people, but their elected representatives. For this reason, the United States is technically not a pure democracy, but a constitutional republic. You also have democratic Parliaments designed to accomplish the same in the free world.

Conservatives at times tend to argue that the constitution should be strengthened, and democracy proportionately weakened. Liberals argue at times for bigger government and yet give lip service to replacing our representative democracy with a direct one. Both are views that stand at the extreme and have been tried before and failed. Both sides of the Political atmosphere have each in their own ways increased spending and made government far bigger than it should be. The Conservatives, though weakened regulations tend to promote the run away banking system that caused our economy to be in trouble. But Liberals on the other hand fostered the atmosphere of give everyone a home along with the their oil production problems that got us here via a one two punch.

For classification purposes, there are three types of society economics: egalitarian, moderated meritocracy, and unrestricted meritocracy.

Socialism is the best example of an egalitarian society. When Marx wrote "From each according to his ability, and to each according to his needs," he was acknowledging that people are certainly born with different abilities, but they should be rewarded equally. It is a system that removes the drive behind industrial growth and wealth.

Libertarianism is the closest example of an unrestricted meritocracy, where there are the fewest constraints on the fittest reaching the top. Unfortunately, we have no historical examples of such a government.

Conservatism and liberalism are examples of moderated meritocracies. In a moderated meritocracy, the most successful continue to be rewarded the most, but a percentage of their power or income is redistributed back to the middle and lower class. Or at least that is supposed to be how it works. The debate between the two is how much redistribution and what for. Both systems utilize the same ends for different outcomes.

In general, the right favors competition; the left, cooperation. The extreme of both sides tends to be in favor of too much competition or cooperation. The first borders on Anarchy and the other on egalitarianism.

Liberalism has a longer history in many ways even going back before the American Revolution. Indeed, as compare to rule under the King of England many of the Founding Father's of this country where themselves in their day Liberals of the old school liberalism in that they saw man's rights and freedoms as something we have from birth and sought to be free from the absolute rule of the King.

Modern Liberalism has its roots in that old school of Liberalism, but it has differed and evolved from that background. Starting with John Keynes, who revolutionized the field of economics. See Classical Liberals such as economist Ludwig von Mises saw that completely Free Markets were the optimal economic units capable of effectively allocating resources so that over time they would achieve full employment and full equality. Keynes, however, argued that totally free markets were not ideal, and that hard economic times required intervention and investment from the state. Where the market failed to properly allocate resources, for example, the government was required to stimulate the economy until private funds could start flowing again—a "prime the pump" kind of strategy designed to boost the economy to the betterment of all. Today's Liberalism has an aspect of this in the more recent bailouts which to be fair was proposed by both the GOP and the Democrats. But the other aspect of Keynes was the idea that not all people are born equal. To Keynes, and many who came after him this violated the spirit of equality and justice. He likened the solution to an Insurance that covered those who where born unable to labor within the free market that made it possible for them to have at least a minimal living standard.

In 1933, when Roosevelt came into office, the unemployment rate was at 25 percent. The size of the economy, measured by the GNP or Gross National Product had fallen to half the value it had in early 1929. The electoral victories of Roosevelt and the Democrats precipitated a vast array of public works programs. Despite this, by 1936 the level of unemployment had only fallen to around 10 percent based upon those in such programs as being employed. Deficit spending sparked by World War II eventually pulled the United States out of the Great Depression. From 1940 to 1941, government spending increased by 59 percent, the GNP rose by 17 percent, and unemployment fell below 10 percent for the first time since 1929. By 1945, after vast government spending, public debit was at 120% of the GNP , but unemployment had been effectively eliminated. The problem one can see from this is that while the Liberal ideal of Government spending to increase employment does achieve that end it also increases the public debit which in the end run has to be paid back. Basically, borrowing from Peter to pay Paul has it's price.

At its very root, liberalism is a philosophy about the meaning of humanity and society. Political philosopher John Grey identified the common strands in liberal thought as being individualist, egalitarian, meliorist, and universalist. The individualist element supports the ethical primacy of the human being against the pressures of Social Collectivism. This runs in principle against the backdrop at the time of Roosevelt of both fascist ideology which emphasized a rejection of equality and Marxism which as a collective State absolute authority sought to level the playing field totally through a Government in absolute control. Both of these had a stern commitment to war as an instrument of natural behavior. However, their means of achieving their goal was different.

At its very root, liberalism is a philosophy about the meaning of humanity and society. It is both that and an idealism of Justice when it comes to humanity and society. The egalitarian element assigns the same moral worth and status to all individuals, the meliorist element asserts that successive generations can improve their sociopolitical arrangements, and the universalist element affirms the moral unity of the human species and marginalizes local cultural differences. The later has been at the heart of many of the Liberal support of both Minority rights, Women's rights, and Gay rights. It has also been at the heart of the problem in dealing with the Middle East which as a whole is not and never has been a society based upon equality. Their refusal to recognize local cultural differences and even more deeply rooted religious law differences makes them blind to the fact that one cannot change at a fundamental level a society that does not want equality. Indeed, upon the very principles outlined by our Founding Father's one could well argue that attempting such change is actually interfering with those in such a regions own right to self choice.

However, not to let Conservatism off the hook many within that camp today have a streak of fascist ideology in that they seek to impose through military conquest the same forced acceptance of something against the free choice of those in that region. Indeed, many of those within the religious right in seeking to impose their idealism of morality via adoption of more laws and changing the educational system in this country seek to do at home what the more Hawkish members of that political group want to do overseas. If we are to remain honest to the founding principles of this Country then none of these extremes is a correct path.

Our Constitution and Bill of Rights was designed so that individual rights should be protected. Society is filled with countless human transactions, each one different, each one changing in the face of new technology, science or social mores. And each one offers a new way for a right to be violated. The same is true of Law in general. What society in the majority thinks at one point in history changes with time. Drinking, Drugs, Homosexuality, Religion come to mind as a few places this is true. Sure Fundamentalist Christians are quick to point out how our Founding Father's idealism was grounded in belief, how our laws are derived from Christian morality. But not every Christian in this country is a Fundamentalists or an Evangelical so even here the interpretation of the moral laws of the Bible are subject to change by the majority in this country even if the Pastors out there do not like that fact. Christianity as far as a established recognized religion has as much variance of viewpoint as when it comes to all this as the political world does.

One other example is there is a growing population in this country that thinks drugs should be legalized, at least some drugs. We see the whole war on drugs no better than an older war on alcohol. If anything the war on drugs actually promotes the crap on our borders people who live along the Mexican border deal with daily. Canada had a similar gang problem till they took away the money these gangs made via legalizing drugs. The whole thing is a free market created problem. Regulate drugs like we try to here and the Gangs and Drug dealers get rich. Legalize them and they have no money to be made. Hell, I'd say legalize Pot and tax the crap out of it like they do Tobacco.

The constitution is only meant to state general principles of governing. It does have to be looked at on an individual case by case instance on weather there is a violation of the rights of people. This holds true for Abortion, Gay rights, etc. It also holds true that our courts have their basis in the Constitution and Bill of Rights. It was not only designed to protect absolute power falling into the hands of one group, but, also to protect us from the same absolute power in our hands as well. Like it or not the courts can override the will of the voters when it comes to what is constitutional or not. The problem is individuals get to interpret the Bill of Rights and the Constitution and people are flawed in how we go about this at times. Today we have a vast divide in this area between those who look at the Constitution as absolute and those who see it as an evolving and living document.

That is the problem in religion and the problem in politics also. Sure the right to bear arms is in the constitution and Bill of Rights. The problem is a militia back then was a people's militia composed of citizens armed to defend their country. Part of the reason that article is there was to protect the people from Government control like we fought to get away from in the first place. The Bill has nothing to do with hunting. It is a Bill to protect our right to defend ourselves and nothing more. The Bill is there to prevent anyone from taking away our right to protect ourselves. But Government can go after those who manufacture arms to prevent certain types of excessive weapons like 40 round pistols from being offered to the public without any actual violation of that Bill. You still have the right to bear arms even if those arms are limited to say 6 to 10 rounds. The Government can establish that criminals cannot bear arms. They can say that you have to be mentally capable to own fire arms. They can run a background check. None of that is a real violation of the right to bear arms. It is all part of promotion of domestic tranquility.

In this day and age thanks to 911 we have a far worse potential rights violation in the way of the Patriot Act. Sure one could argue that even though it allows without warrant our government to wire tap us that such has not actually happened. But the problem is the Constitution and the Bill of Rights forbids our government that power even if it is only a potential one. Sure they can argue it promotes domestic tranquility but it also is a direct violation of the Constitution no matter how you look at it. It also promotes the crap people and parents are putting up with daily at our airports and is at the heart of a debate in Texas recently where the Transportation Security agency of the Government basically trampled on States rights and said they would stop all flights into and out of Texas if the State voted to outlaw body searches by them. And these same idiots wonder why some States talk about dropping out of the Union. States have rights too as well as the individual. Sure we live in a world with people out there hell bent on our destruction. But if the rights of the people are being violated to achieve safety is that safety worth abandonment of the Bill of Rights and the Constitution?

That is the Big question few voters have bothered to even pay attention too. A right once given is very hard to ever get back. Most democracy has failed in history with acceptance of the taking away of certain rights. It fails under applause not tears. Hitler took power by right sounding promises, not by saying he was going to rule the land with an iron fist.

Contrary to what the First Amendment says, many forms of speech are outlawed in this country. Examples include slander, libel, perjury, insider-trading, malicious deceptions, impersonating an officer, revealing classified information, making bomb jokes in an airport, etc. Our News media leaking classified information during a war on the location of our troops is one good example of the limit under the law to freedom of the Press. We are a Nation of Law before anything else. This is the heart and soul of the debate over torture as a means to get information from the enemy. It is also the heart and soul over the other debates like Gay Marriage and abortion. But here again the Laws tend to change with time and are subject to debate as well as interpretation.

Sure our Founding Fathers said, rights are natural, self-evident and God-given. But the interpretation of the meaning of those rights is up to the courts of our land who themselves like us are flawed. Only when something is clear cut can they act with out the need to interpret.

Congress by the vote of the people through their representatives could enact a law tomorrow that says Gay Marriage is forbidden. But if the Supreme Court of this country decided that was not constitutional then that law would become null and void. Congress can enact laws to limit abortion. But it is the right of the Supreme Court to determine if those limits violate the Constitution. Both of these arguments that exist belong in the hands of the Courts and not Congressional Leaders like it or not. Only the Courts have that right to determine on those issues, not the Church and not the Congress, nor the President either.

We have separation of Church and State for a reason in this country. No more Religious Dictatorship and no King in America. We have the right to worship as we please here even if the way we worship and the one we worship is not the Fundamentalists idea of God. Vote your conscience, yes. But do not try to dictate everyone else's morality has to follow your idea of such. Let the damn courts work the way they where designed to work instead of trying to micromanage the morality of every American. Be the Salt of the earth in you're conversation and lives. But quit trying to be a bitter root in everyone else's life. You never saw Christ once speak out against the Government. In fact he said render under Caesar what is Caesar's. But he sure had a lot to say about the religious leaders of his day and none of it was good. I suspect he'd have the same things to say about most of our religious leaders today. The Movie Oh God had it right about Minister's having quit preaching God's word long ago. I'd also say a lot of those in Political Power quit following the will of the People long ago also.

Most Christians know only one Biblical reason to oppose abortion, and that is the obvious one, "Thou shalt not kill." This is one of the most critical laws a society can obey, and every pro-choice advocate agrees with it. However, it is impossible to break this commandment if there is no person on the receiving end of this action. The question concerns what we as a Nation define as life. Is an unborn baby at conception a living breathing person is the central issue. If that Baby is then that baby has rights under our constitution. The problem is there is no solid consensus even amongst the religious community. And the medical community itself has offered no solid answer here either.

The Hebrew word for "kill" in the 6th Commandment is rasach, which more accurately means "murder," or illegal killing judged harmful by the community. It is itself a relative term! Many forms of killing were considered legal; indeed, God often gave Israel permission to kill. (In I Samuel 15:3, God ordered Saul to massacre the Amalekites: "Do not spare them; put to death men and women, children and infants...") Generally, levitical law permits killing in times of war, the commission of justice and in self-defense. And so does our own laws of the land in many ways. We just got done killing Ben Laden and few in this country would see that as not a justified killing.

Jewish law is quite clear in its statement that an embryo is not reckoned a viable living thing (in Hebrew, bar kayama) until thirty days after its birth. Prior to that it is not a living being protected by the same rights as a living person. A fetus is not considered a person under Jewish law, it would be impossible to consider its abortion a murder. Most Jewish scholars have agreed that abortion was legal under Jewish law. The root of most of our law here in America goes back to the Old Testament and Jewish Law. According to the first book of the Bible God first formed Adam from the dust of the ground, and only then did he give him the breath of life, turning man into a living soul. This similar to the scientific description of pregnancy, which notes that the first seven months are devoted to constructing the organs and body, and only by the 8th month does the fetus display a waking consciousness. The Body that is supposed to house the soul under Christian thought is not fully formed in the early stages of conception during which most abortions are carried out.

In Exodus 21:22-23:
> "If men who are fighting hit a pregnant woman and she gives birth prematurely but there is no serious injury [i.e., to the mother], the offender must be fined whatever the woman's husband demands and the court allows. But if there is serious injury [i.e., to the mother], you are to take life for life, eye for eye, tooth for tooth, hand for hand, foot for foot..."

The Body of a baby has always even in the Bible been looked at differently from an already born and living human being.

The First Amendment states:
> "Congress shall make no law respecting an establishment of religion, or prohibiting the free exercise thereof..."

Basically that is rather self evident. No established religion by the State and no prohibiting of the free exercise of a religion. That means Christians, Hindus, Buddhists, Taoists, atheists, agnostics,Wiccans and those of Islamic faith are free to worship God as they feel fit and not even the Government can tell them how to do so. We have no State established religion in this country even if a lot of the Founding Fathers where Christian. In fact, they made sure being religious was not a requirement to work in the Government also. They where students of history and knew religious organizations can hinder freedom of the people as much a corrupt Government can. In fact, a some of the Founding Fathers where Deists more than anything else.

This famous phrase was coined by Thomas Jefferson in his letter to the Danbury Baptists:
> "Believing that religion is a matter which lies solely between man and his God, that he owes account to none other for his faith or his worship, that the legislative powers of government reach actions only, and not opinions, I contemplate with sovereign reverence that act of the whole American people which declared that their Legislature

should 'make no law respecting an establishment of religion, or prohibiting the free exercise thereof,' thus building a wall of separation between Church and State." -- Thomas Jefferson to Danbury Baptists, 1802.

This really shows what one of the Founding Father's thought about the place of religion and Politics. Believing that religion is a matter which lies solely between man and his God would go a long way towards shutting up the religious moral majority in this country if it was practiced today. Instead they want to shove their idealism down the throats of every America Citizen and if they had their way the same would be forced taught to all of our children. It is the Church and the Parents God given right to teach such. Not the damn state controlled by religious bigots.

I believe in Science and I am glad my children can learn freely what science has to say. But I also believe in a Creator and support the right of every parent to pass on to their children what they believe. I do not need some Religious right winger telling me what my kids should believe or not believe. I do not want Creationism rammed down in the minds any more than I want pure Atheism either. I want them to look at the evidence science has to offer, to hear all sides and make a choice of their own the same choice I made myself. They hear all sides from me as a Parent and from any Church or religion they themselves choice to attend. Not from Creationism being taught in our schools. Our Public schools should remain secular as should our State. I will vote for a Christian as quick as a non-Christian. I vote for the person, not his belief. But I will never vote a Minster of any faith into office. I could never trust such a person to actually represent all of Americans.

One of the first proponents of Conservatism was Russell Kirk in his book published in 1953 The Conservative Mind. Basically, Conservatism arose after the 20 year term of Franklin Roosevelt who had blamed Conservative ideals on many of the problems that lead to World War Two. Basically, like today's GOP, Kirk saw the religious roots as the backbone of Conservatism. He sought slow change and not radical utopian idealism. Like many in the Libertarian side today he saw Property rights as the basis of true Freedom. Though Libertarianism has its roots more back in the idealism of Robert Nozick who disagreed with John Rawls who emphasized the need to ensure not only equality under the law, but also the equal distribution of material resources that individuals required to develop their aspirations in life which is the current idealism of Liberalism. Nozick followed more after a Lockean idealism.

Later, Willmoore Kendall wrote his own ideas of Conservatism in a rebuttal of Kirk's ideas. This split remains mixed even to today within the Conservative Movement. It is even more interesting how the anti-war crowd of the 70's within the Democratic Party drove the Hawks from that Party into the GOP where they have tended to stay till today and has brought about a strong influence from this group when it comes to support of the Military/Industrial Complex. Certainly both Ronald Reagan and both Bush's where influenced by this part of the Conservative Movement. But all of these represent divisions within what on the outside seems like a solid unitary Movement.

In some ways there has developed a sort of trinity between the social conservatives, the fiscal conservatives, and those of a more Lockean leaning. The problem is that trinity has begun to splinter apart due to the influence of the Lockean camp and due to the fact that a lot of the more Independent supporters of the Conservatives are more fiscally so and far less social conservatives. In some ways the Libertarians of today where the Liberals back in the 60's and the Independents of today are fiscal conservatives with roots of their own back in the original liberal idealism. These two groups have far more in common than they hold with either Party at present and could well hold the key to development of an eventual third party in this country.

This Nation is founded upon a general body of law designed to protect us from exactly what we have going on in this Country today. We fought the war of Independence to escape taxation without representation, we fought that war long ago to escape religious persecution from any one group, our Fore Father's added in a Bill of Rights to protect the freedoms they found dear enough to lay down their lives over and saw fit in the very declaration of their break with England to give us warning of what happens when those freedoms are taken away.

But 236 years later those warnings go ignored by many of our Leaders who are supposed to represent us, by the religious leaders who seem more interested in growing government control of reproduction, education with vouchers for religious run schools, forced mandates on health insurance, bail out of the banking industry and Big Corporations, and unconstitutional laws like NDAA, the Patriot Act, etc. Basically, while 99% of this country struggles to make a living the 1% out there has managed to do away with any pretense of real democracy and grow their own wealth and power in the process. It is to this 1% and those that are really behind the public eye in them that the rest of this book is addressed.

THE ROOTS OF THE DARK FORCES

There are two groups of elite men and women in particular that most American people do not know about, but which are a clear threat and danger to the freedom of the American people. These are the Council on Foreign Relations (CFR) and the Trilateral Commission. Right now the United States is completely under the control of those who run these two organizations. It is therefore important to understand these organizations if we wish to understand what has been taking place in the United States since the early 1900's.

In 1921, House and his friends formed the Council on Foreign Relations whose purpose right from its conception was to destroy the freedom and independence of the United States, and to lead the country into a one-world government. Right from its beginning, in 1921, the CFR began to attract men of power and influence. In the late 1920's, important financing for the CFR came from the Rockefeller Foundation and the Carnegie Foundation. In 1940, at the invitation of President Roosevelt, members of the CFR gained domination over the State Department, and they have maintained this domination ever since.

The CFR is the American Branch of a society which originated in England, and which believes that national boundaries should be obliterated, and a one-world rule established." statement by Carroll Quigley, mentor of men like Bill Clinton and other major members of both parties in this country. It has fostered this belief both through the promotion and adaptation of Liberalism and Conservatism to it's own ends. While strongly supporting both large multinational Corporations, World banking through the IMF, and the Oil Industry, it has used it's liberal members to promote socialistic goals, not of the more traditional type, but, more with a goal of Corporatism being the central avenue of control of both the means of production and the general population as a whole. Basically, if you control the Banks and you control all the goods the world needs you own the world.

Many have spoken out over time against the CFR. Rear Admiral Chester Ward, a former member of the CFR for 16 years, warned the American people of the organization's intentions:
"The most powerful clique in these elitist groups have one objective in common — they want to bring about the surrender of the sovereignty of the national independence of the United States. A second clique of international members in the CFR comprises the Wall Street international bankers and their key agents. Primarily, they want the world banking

monopoly from whatever power ends up in the control of global government."

What he was warning us about was the two fold program these elitist groups have as their agenda.   They want to destroy America's Independence and they want control of the World Banking system. They really do not care who Nation wise is the main power player. In fact, they'd just as soon see the world divided up as long as they control all sides.

Dan Smoot, a former member of the FBI Headquarters staff in Washington, D.C., summarized the organization's purpose as follows:
"The ultimate aim of the CFR is to create a one-world socialist system, and to make the U.S. an official part of it."   They are after Global Control of everything to do with our lives. This organization owns the big business and Federal Reserve and Banks that control and bankroll both of our political systems. President, Thomas Dewey, was a CFR member. In later years, Republicans Eisenhower and Nixon were members of the CFR, as were Democrats Stevenson, Kennedy, Humphrey, and McGovern. Clinton and Bush are members of the Trilateral Council. More on that in a moment. Obama is not a member, but most of his major staff is. NBC and CBS, 'The New York Times', 'The Washington Post', 'The Des Moines Register', and many other important newspapers. The leaders of 'Time', 'Newsweek', 'Fortune', 'Business Week', and numerous other publications are CFR members. Given Bane Capital's connection itself, you can add in Clear channel which hosts most of the Talk show hosts and even Fox into all that. It is an express condition of membership that no one is to disclose what goes on at CFR meetings, but a few have talked and leaked documents over the years. They have people in all the major religious organizations.

Basically, they own every aspect that affects our lives.

The Trilateral Commission is a non-governmental, non-partisan discussion group founded by David Rockefeller in July 1973, to foster closer cooperation among the United States, Europe and Japan.
- Growing interdependence is a fact of life of the contemporary world. It transcends and influences national systems...While it is important to develop greater cooperation among all the countries of the world, Japan, Western Europe, and North America, in view of their great weight in the world economy and their massive relations with one another, bear a special responsibility for developing effective cooperation, both in their own interests and in those of the rest of the world."
- "To be effective in meeting common problems, Japan, Western Europe, and North America will have to consult and cooperate more closely, on the basis of equality, to develop and carry out coordinated policies on matters affecting their common interests...refrain from unilateral actions incompatible with their interdependence and from actions detrimental to other regions... [and] take advantage of existing international and regional organizations and further enhance their role."
- "The Commission hopes to play a creative role as a channel of free exchange of

opinions with other countries and regions. Further progress of the developing countries and greater improvement of East-West relations will be a major concern."[1]

Zbigniew Brzezinski, a professor at Columbia University and a Rockefeller advisor who was a specialist on international affairs, left his post to organize the group along with:

- Henry D. Owen (a Foreign Policy Studies Director with the Brookings Institution)
- George S. Franklin
- Robert R. Bowie (of the Foreign Policy Association and Director of the Harvard Center for International Affairs)
- Gerard C. Smith (Salt I negotiator, Rockefeller in-law, and its first North American Chairman)
- Marshall Hornblower (former partner at Wilmer, Cutler & Pickering)
- William Scranton (former Governor of Pennsylvania)
- Edwin Reischauer (a professor at Harvard)
- Max Kohnstamm (European Policy Centre)

Other founding members included Alan Greenspan and Paul Volcker, both later heads of the Federal Reserve system.

The IMF has 187 member countries. It is a specialized agency of the United Nations but has its own charter, governing structure, and finances.

The World Trade Organization (WTO) is the only global international organization dealing with the rules of trade between nations. At its heart are the WTO agreements, negotiated and signed by the bulk of the world's trading nations and ratified in their parliaments. The goal is to help producers of goods and services, exporters, and importers conduct their business. But this also leaves them in the unique position of control of the goods and services worldwide.

The effects of the Council on Foreign Relation and The Trilateral Commission on the affaires of our nation is easy to see. Our own Government no longer acts in its own interest, we no longer win any wars we fight, and we constantly tie ourselves to international agreements, pacts, and conventions. And, our leaders have developed blatant preferences for Russia., Communist Cuba, and Communist China, while they continue to work for world government, which has always been the goal of Communism and socialism. They have for decades had a plan to take over step by step the wealth of the Middle East. Good modern example is Libya. We did not return that money we seized during their rebellion. The WMF and banking groups gave them loans based on those funds that have to be paid back with interest even though basically the industry structure was destroyed during all those bombings, and the money their country had in oil was what this organization used. Same with Iraq and Afghanistan. Every dollar given is in form of loans with interest due. Part of their plan has always been using the US in small wars to basically carve up countries that would require force to take over.

All the documents on this are out there. The Charters are public record as our certain laws claimed to protect freedom that have gutted our Bill of Rights and the Constitution.

Barry Goldwater, the first Conservative of major import warned about them. Their methods are simple: Divide and take over. Get everyone at each others throats, get Government in a stalemate and simply take over.

Dr. Henry Kissinger made an odd quote once to the Trilateral Council that today if the UN landed military on the US everyone would rise up in arms. He went on to say 20 years from now they will welcome you. Freedom and Liberty die not with sadness. It dies with approval, ignorance, and clapping of hands. At the current time as I write this we have Foreign Troops on our soil in several major cities. These are Russian Troops here for the backdrop of leaning how to fight terrorists. But irrespective of the reason they are here you do not hear anyone up in arms over their being here at all. In that aspect Kissinger was dead right. The sleeping sheep most American's have become have gotten used to this global world that the CFR worked to set up and pay little attention to anything going on around them. Not much of a step one could say from UN Troops landing on our soil to help with say a major outbreak of our equal to the Arab Spring.

The evidence as I say is out there if one simply opens your eyes and begins to take a look around. But given that most of the original members of the CFR are long gone the one big question is who is running all this. Every organization has a structure and somewhere within that structure there is someone at the top in control. One can run down a list of CFR members, Trilateral Members, WMF Members, etc. But, while you can find the connection between all these different groups you cannot find that one person in control. The same was true back in the 1920's. Even then, though you had certain key figures who appeared in many of the agency groups involved. You had no dominate person in control. Yet, somewhere away from the public eye such a figure has to exist.

Yes, I know you are going to say that they could be set up a lot like the Terrorists in that you have several key spokes people, power players if you wish. But if you eliminate one the movement just sprouts up again. The problem is for such a wide spread organization they have to be taking marching orders from a central control. You could think of it as a virus which to multiply has to duplicate its DNA. The central control would be that DNA without which there could be no order to the system. Even if there is no at present one key leader there still has to be a center of control. And that center of control is the one key element of these Dark Forces that has left almost nothing to go on.

Even more in favor of there being a central control is found in some of the Trilateral Commission's own words back at it's founding: "The Commission hopes to play a creative role as a channel of free exchange of opinions with other countries and regions. Further progress of the developing countries and greater improvement of East-West relations will be a major concern." This East-West issue takes on an interesting light given the fall of Communism in Russia partly brought about by Military buildup under Reagan putting vast pressure on their monetary system. Now we have former enemy soldiers on our soil learning from us. Another member of the East, China has itself adapted a controlled version of Capitalism and has major treaties with us. So who or what is in charge is an important question given how far the goals of these Agents of change have gone.

One of it's founding members had a lot to say, "Some even believe we (the Rockefeller family) are part of a secret cabal working against the best interests of the United States, characterizing my family and me as 'internationalists' and of conspiring with others around the world to build a more integrated global political and economic structure – one world, if you will. If that's the charge, I stand guilty, and I am proud of it."
- David Rockefeller, Memoirs, page 405

Even more recent we have,

"In the next century, nations as we know it will be obsolete; all states will recognize a single, global authority. National sovereignty wasn't such a great idea after all."
- Strobe Talbot, President Clinton's Deputy Secretary of State, Time Magazine, July 20th, 1992

"There does exist, and has existed for a generation, an international anglophile network which operates, to some extent, in the way the radical Right believes the Communists act. In fact, this network, which we may identify as the Round Table Groups, has no aversion to cooperating with the communists, or any other group, and frequently does so. I know of the operations of this network because I have studied it for twenty years and was permitted for two years, in the early 1960s, to examine its papers and secret records. I have no aversion to it or to most of its aims and have, for much of my life, been close to it and to many of its instruments … I have objected both in the past and recently, to a few of its policies … but in general my chief difference of opinion is that it wishes to remain unknown, and I believe its role in history is significant enough to be known … The Council on Foreign Relations (CFR) … the American Branch of a society which originated in England … believes national boundaries should be obliterated and [a] one-world rule established."
Prof. Carroll Quigley, mentor to Bill Clinton, from his book 'Tragedy and Hope'

"Ultimately, our objective is to welcome the Soviet Union back into the world order. Perhaps the world order of the future will truly be a family of nations."
President George Bush at Texas A&M University 1989

"We will succeed in the Gulf. And when we do, the world community will have sent an enduring warning to any dictator or despot, present or future, who contemplates outlaw aggression. The world can therefore seize this opportunity to fufill the long-held promise of a new world order – where brutality will go unrewarded, and aggression will meet collective resistance."
President George Bush State of the Union Address 1991

"The Final Act of the Uruguay Round, marking the conclusion of the most ambitious trade negotiation of our century, will give birth – in Morocco – to the World Trade

Organization, the third pillar of the New World Order, along with the United Nations and the International Monetary Fund."
Part of full-page advertisement by the government of Morocco in The New York Times (April 1994)

"What Congress will have before it is not a conventional trade agreement but the architecture of a new international system...a first step toward a new world order."
Henry Kissinger on NAFTA, Los Angeles Times

"All these new challenges are bringing together about the biggest restructuring we've ever seen not just of the global economy but global order as a whole. And two hundred years ago, a famous British foreign secretary said that the new world had been called into existence to address the balance of the old. In 1989 another world war ended dominated by the cold war and people talked then in 1990 of the new world order. What they meant then was a new political order. And what was not foreseen then but is obvious now, from everything that we see and do, what we experience every day of our life is the sheer scale and speed and scope of globalization..."
Prime Minister Gordon Brown, CBI Speech 2007

"The New World Order will have to be built from the bottom up rather than from the top down...but in the end run around national sovereignty, eroding it piece by piece will accomplish much more than the old fashioned frontal assault."
CFR member Richard Gardner, writing in the April 1974 issue of the CFR's journal, Foreign Affairs

"The Final Act of the Uruguay Round, marking the conclusion of the most ambitious trade negotiation of our century, will give birth – in Morocco – to the World Trade Organization, the third pillar of the New World Order, along with the United Nations and the International Monetary Fund."
Part of full-page advertisement by the government of Morocco in The New York Times (April 1994)

If one simply takes a look at:

http://www.hudson.org/files/pdf_upload/HudsonNegotiatingNorthAmericaadvanceproof2.pdf

You will see that the Security and Prosperity Partnership agreement between Canada, the U.S., and Mexico, was designed to dissolve sovereign military and economic functions between the three countries. I could also point out the recent training of the Iranian dissident group Mujahideen-e-Khalq (MEK) at a secretive Department of Energy site in Nevada:

http://www.newyorker.com/online/blogs/newsdesk/2012/04/mek.html

All of this is public knowledge. Yet, the majority of American's sit back, conditioned by the Education system under their control at many levels, the media bought and sold by them, and those in High Office under their fiscal control and believe this is all just BS or worse "conspiracy theorists" BS. The Problem is if you honestly do the research this is anything but "conspiracy theory". In fact, it is a nightmare that unfolds daily around us with most American's sitting back like sheep on the way to slaughter.

For those of you thinking FOX News tells the truth you might want to know that Rupert Murdoch and Deroy Murdock both are members of CFR and their own organization developed and owns Fox. Rather brings into question their whole Fair and Balanced motto.

Who then are some of the other members of this organization?

Board of Directors of the CFR

Carla A. Hills
Co-Chairman; Chairman and CEO, Hills & Company
Robert E. Rubin
Co-Chairman; Former Secretary of the U.S. Treasury
Richard E. Salomon
Vice Chairman; Managing Partner, East End Advisors, LLC
Richard N. Haass
President, Council on Foreign Relations
John P. Abizaid
Senior Partner, JPA Partners LLC
Peter Ackerman
Managing Director, Rockport Capital, Inc.
Fouad Ajami
Senior Fellow, Hoover Institution, Stanford University
Madeleine K. Albright
Chair, Albright Stonebridge Group LLC
Alan S. Blinder
Gordon S. Rentschler Memorial Professor of Economics and Public Affairs, Princeton University
Mary Boies
Managing Partner, Boies & McInnis LLP
David G. Bradley
Chairman, Atlantic Media Company
Tom Brokaw
Special Correspondent, NBC News
Sylvia Mathews Burwell

Host, CNN's Fareed Zakaria GPS

Officers

Carla A. Hills
Co-Chairman

Robert E. Rubin
Co-Chairman

Richard E. Salomon
Vice Chairman

Richard N. Haass
President

Keith Olson
Executive Vice President, Chief Financial Officer, and Treasurer

David Kellogg
Chief Information Officer and Publisher

James M. Lindsay
Senior Vice President, Director of Studies, and Maurice R. Greenberg Chair

Nancy D. Bodurtha
Vice President, Meetings

Irina A. Faskianos
Vice President, National Program and Outreach

Suzanne E. Helm
Vice President, Development

Jan Mowder Hughes
Vice President, Human Resources and Administration

L. Camille Massey
Vice President, Membership, Corporate, and International

Lisa Shields
Vice President, Communications and Marketing

Jeffrey A. Reinke
Secretary of the Corporation

Officers and Directors, Emeritus & Honorary

Leslie H. Gelb
President Emeritus

Maurice R. Greenberg
Honorary Vice Chairman

Peter G. Peterson
Chairman Emeritus

David Rockefeller
Honorary Chairman

On the Corporate Side:

Founders

Bank of America Merrill Lynch
Chevron Corporation
Exxon Mobil Corporation
Goldman Sachs Group, Inc.
Hess Corporation
JPMorgan Chase & Co
McKinsey & Company, Inc.
The Nasdaq OMX Group
President's Circle
Alcoa, Inc.
American Express
Barclays Capital
Bennett Jones LLP
BP p.l.c.
Bridgewater Associates, LP
CA Technologies
Citi
Credit Suisse
Dell Inc.
Eni
Fortress Investment Group LLC
GoldenTree Asset Management
Guardsmark LLC
Kingdon Capital Management
Kohlberg Kravis Roberts & Co.
Korn/Ferry International
Lazard
Lockheed Martin Corporation
Mars, Inc.
McGraw-Hill Companies, The
MetLife
Moody's Corporation
Morgan Stanley
New Media Investments
Omnicom Group Inc.
Parsons Corporation
Reliance Industries Limited
Shell Oil Company
Soros Fund Management
Standard Chartered Bank
The AES Corporation
Toyota Motor North America, Inc.
Veritas Capital LLC
Weiss Multi-Strategy Advisors, LLC
ACE Limited

Airbus Americas, Inc.
Allen & Overy LLP
Allied World Assurance Company, Ltd.
Apollo Management, LP
Aramco Services Company
AREVA Inc.
Arnhold and S. Bleichroeder Holdings, Inc.
Arnold & Porter LLP
AT&T
Baker Capital Corp.
Baker, Nye Advisers, Inc.
Baldwin-Gottschalk Group, The
Banco Mercantil
Bank of New York Mellon Corporation, The
BASF Corporation
BGR Group
Bingham McCutchen LLP
Blackstone Group L.P., The
Bloomberg
BNP Paribas
Boeing Company, The
Booz Allen Hamilton Inc.
Bunge Limited
Canadian Imperial Bank of Commerce
Caterpillar
Caxton Associates
Chartis
Cisneros Group of Companies
CIT Group Inc.
Clarium Capital Management, LLC
Cleary Gottlieb Steen & Hamilton LLP
CNA
Coca-Cola Company, The
ConocoPhillips Company
Continental Properties
Control Risks Group
Corsair Capital
Covington & Burling
Craig Drill Capital Corporation
Crédit Agricole Corporate and Investment Bank
De Beers
Deere & Company
Deloitte.
Deutsche Bank AG
Duke Energy Corporation

DynCorp International
Economist Intelligence Unit
Energy Intelligence Group, Inc.
Equinox Partners, L.P.
Estee Lauder Companies Inc.
Federal Express Corporation
Freeport-McMoRan Copper and Gold Inc.
Future Pipe Industries, Inc.
General Atlantic LLC
General Electric Company
Gibson, Dunn & Crutcher, LLP
GlaxoSmithKline
Google, Inc.
Granite Associates LP
Greenberg Traurig, LLP
Hitachi, Ltd.
IBM Corporation
Indus Capital Partners, LLC
Intesa Sanpaolo
Invus Group, LLC
ITOCHU International
Jacobs Asset Management, LLC
Kroll
MacAndrews & Forbes Holdings Inc.
Mannheim LLC
Marsh & McLennan Companies, Inc.
Marubeni America Corporation
MBIA Insurance Corporation
MeadWestvaco Corporation
Merck & Co., Inc.
Microsoft Corporation
Milbank, Tweed, Hadley & McCloy LLP
Mitsubishi Heavy Industries America, Inc.
Mitsubishi International Corporation
Mitsui & Co. (U.S.A.), Inc.
Moore Capital Management LLC
News Corporation, The
Northrop Grumman
NYSE Euronext
Occidental Petroleum Corporation
Olayan Group, The
PepsiCo, Inc.
Pfizer Inc.
PricewaterhouseCoopers LLP (PwC)
Principal Financial Group

Prudential Financial
Raytheon Company
Rho Capital Partners
Rothschild North America, Inc.
Sandalwood Securities, Inc.
Siguler Guff & Company L.P.
Silver Lake Partners
Simpson Thacher & Bartlett LLP
Sony Corporation of America
Standard & Poor's
Sullivan & Cromwell LLP
T. Rowe Price Group
Tata Group, The
Telefonica Internacional U.S.A.
Thomson Reuters
TIAA-CREF
Time Warner Inc.
Tishman Speyer Properties, Inc.
TOTAL S.A.
U.S. Chamber of Commerce
UBS AG
United Technologies Corporation
Verizon Communications
Volkswagen Group of America, Inc.
Vornado Realty Trust
Walmart
Warburg Pincus LLC
Wyoming Investment LLC
Xerox Corporation
Zephyr Management, L.P.
Ziff Brothers Investments LLC
AARP
Banca d'Italia
Hemispheric Partners
Japan Bank for International Cooperation
Oxford Analytica Inc.

Just that little bit reads like a who's who in the Wall Street, Banking, and Big Business World. It also shows just how far a reach they have into every human being on the Planet's life. And that is just a surface list of Members connected with the CFR.

If you think the Tea Party, backed by the Koch brothers is out of this loop wait and read the next. Fred Koch (1900-1967) was a chemical engineer who invented a new process for refining oil. Supposedly, he was shut out of the US by the Rockefellers and had to go to work for Stalin. He built many refineries in Soviet Russia and trained Russian engineers to operate them. Supposedly, he became disillusioned with Communism and became a founding member of the John Birch Society in the 1950's.

The trouble is that according to the 1964-65, Edition of Who's Who, this militant anti-Communist was still building refineries in Russia and Eastern Europe. Moreover, the John Birch society was <u>founded by members of the Council on Foreign Relations</u>, many of whom were Masons, and staffed by former Communist writers.

<u>Koch Industries</u> is the second-largest private company in America after Cargill. "With an annual revenue of $100 billion, the company was just $6.3 billion shy of first place in 2008. Ownership is kept strictly in the family, with the company being split roughly between brothers Charles and David Koch, who are worth about $20 billion apiece...Today, it operates thousands of miles of pipelines in the United States, refines 800,000 barrels of crude oil daily, buys and sells the most asphalt in the nation, is among the top 10 cattle producers, and is among the 50 largest landowners." But they have their roots deep into the Council on Foreign Relations and while favoring Free Market, still has a questionable Business. Koch Industries owns Brawny paper towels, Dixie cups, Georgia-Pacific lumber, Stainmaster carpet, and Lycra, among other products."

According to Yasha Levine who did research about them :

"William Koch, the third brother who had a falling-out with Charles and David back in the '80s over Charles' sociopathic management style, appeared on "60 Minutes" in November 2000 to tell the world that Koch Industries was a criminal enterprise: "It was - was my family company. I was out of it," he says. "But that's what appalled me so much... I did not want my family, my legacy, my father's legacy to be based upon organized crime." "Charles Koch's racket was very simple," explained William. "With its extensive oil pipe network, Koch Industries' role as an oil middleman--it buys crude from someone's well and sells it to a refinery--makes it easy to steal millions of dollars worth of oil by skimming just a little off the top of each transaction, or what they call "cheating measurements" in the oil trade. According to William, wells located on federal and Native American lands were the prime targets of the Koch scam.

In May 2008, a unit of <u>Koch Industries</u> Inc., one of the world's largest privately held companies, sent Ludmila Egorova-Farines, its newly hired compliance officer and ethics manager, to investigate the management of a subsidiary in Arles in southern France. In less than a week, she discovered that the company had paid bribes to win contracts.

"I uncovered the practices within a few days," Egorova-Farines says. "They were not hidden at all."

She immediately notified her supervisors in the U.S. A week later, Wichita, Kansas-based Koch Industries dispatched an investigative team to look into her findings, Bloomberg Markets magazine reports in its November issue.

By September of that year, the researchers had found evidence of improper payments to secure contracts in six countries dating back to 2002, authorized by the business director of the company's Koch-Glitsch affiliate in France.

"Those activities constitute violations of criminal law,"Koch Industries wrote in a Dec. 8, 2008, letter giving details of its findings. The letter was made public in a civil court ruling in France in September 2010; the document has never before been reported by the media.

Egorova-Farines wasn't rewarded for bringing the illicit payments to the company's attention. Her superiors removed her from the inquiry in August 2008 and fired her in June 2009, calling her incompetent, even after Koch's investigators substantiated her findings. She sued Koch-Glitsch in France for wrongful termination.

A Bloomberg Markets investigation has found that Koch Industries was involved in improper payments to win business in Africa, India and the Middle East and has sold millions of dollars of petrochemical equipment to Iran, a country the U.S. identifies as a sponsor of global terrorism. So in essence, while they back the Tea Party in this Country they sell US interests off to those who would destroy America.

Internal company documents show that the company made those sales through foreign subsidiaries, thwarting a U.S. trade ban. Koch Industries units have also rigged prices with competitors, lied to regulators and repeatedly run afoul of environmental regulations, resulting in five criminal convictions since 1999 in the U.S. and Canada.

From 1999 through 2003, Koch Industries was assessed more than $400 million in fines, penalties and judgments. In December 1999, a civil jury found that Koch Industries had taken oil it didn't pay for from federal land by mismeasuring the amount of crude it was extracting. Koch paid a $25 million settlement to the U.S.

Phil Dubose, a Koch employee who testified against the company said he and his colleagues were shown by their managers how to steal and cheat using what he said they term to Koch Method backing up much of their separated Brother's claims about the Company.

Sally Barnes-Soliz, who's now an investigator for the State Department of Labor and Industries in Washington, says that when she worked for Koch, her bosses and a company lawyer at the Koch refinery in Corpus Christi, Texas, asked her to falsify data for a report to the state on uncontrolled emissions of benzene, a known cause of cancer. Barnes-Soliz, who testified to a federal grand jury, says she refused to alter the numbers.
"They didn't know what to do with me," she says. "They were really kind of baffled that I had ethics."

Koch's refinery unit pleaded guilty in 2001 to a federal felony charge of lying to regulators and paid $20 million in fines and penalties.

The Senate held hearings in May 1989 after <u>Bill Koch</u>, David Koch's twin brother, told a U.S. Senate special committee on investigations that Koch Industries was stealing oil on American Indian reservations, cheating the federal government of royalties.
Bill Koch had a long-standing feud with his brothers after his failed attempt to take over the company in the early 1980s. He sold his shares in June 1983 and later lost a lawsuit claiming he'd been shortchanged.

The Senate committee sent investigators to Oklahoma to secretly observe oil companies, including Koch, buying crude on Indian land. The federal agents hid in ditches, crouched behind scrub cedars and ducked behind cows to avoid detection by Koch Oil's purchasers, FBI agent Richard Elroy testified to the committee in May 1989.

The investigators caught Koch Oil's employees falsifying records so that the company would get more crude than it paid for, shortchanging Indian families, Elroy said. Koch's records showed that the company took 1.95 million barrels of oil it didn't pay for from 1986 to 1988, according to data compiled by the Senate.

One begins in all this to see a pattern and why they are so anti-government. They make their profit out of being anything but supportive of American Law and Government. But they have learned how to build wealth while robbing from everyone they can. These same Brothers have control of the Tea Party via that same stolen money and have attempted at all avenues to literally fight for their own share of the rising New World Order through ever means possible. Yet, it is ironic that the Party they Fund would even dare use the name Tea Party given it was robbery of another type that lead our Fore Father's in Boston so long ago to throw tea into the Bay.

THE RELIGIOUS RIGHT AND THE CFR

The Religious Right, through groups like the Southern Baptists Convention, certain Oneness Pentecostals, and others have their connection to the Council on Foreign Relations. Recently Richard Land, president and CEO of the Southern Baptist Convention Ethics & Religious Liberty Commission, and Rick Warren, a mega-church pastor and author of The Purpose Driven Life, are on record as belonging to the Council on Foreign Relations.

Land spoke to the group in 2005 on evangelicals and the Middle East. Warren has also addressed the group, presenting his global plan to enlist Christians in the fight against poverty, illiteracy and AIDS. Some other religious Leaders with ties include, Rev. Sun Myung Moon, Tim LaHaye, Paul Crouch, Bill Bright, Rev. Billy Graham, Jay Sekulow, all through the Moon sponsored organization the Council of National Policy founded in 1981 by Tim LaHaye. One can also add in Political Leaders like Senators Jesse Helms, Don Nickles, and Trent Lott. Also Representatives Tom DeLay, Dan Burton, and Bob Dornan to name a few. Another past President of CNP is Rich DeVoss, co-founder of Amway. When you add in the World Council of Churches under the UN you bring in not only the Roman Catholic Church, but many other main World Religions including Islam. But the one in American today with the strongest influence in Politics is the Religious Right which itself has these Dark Forces at work within it's many organizations.

Here in America alone we have:

American Freedom Coalition
Led by Dr. Robert Grant and also a Moonie funded organization. In a period of a little

over 2 years they received nearly 6 million dollars from Moon organizations and enterprises. This group includes Paul Crouch, Rex Humbard, James Robinson and many more, names well known among the evangelical Christian community.

Concerned Women of America
Headed by Beverly LaHaye. The wife of Tim LaHaye, She too has been a public speaker for Moon functions.

Womens Federation for World Peace
Also headed by Beverly LaHaye and recipient of Moon funding. Former President George Bush Sr. (and one time former CIA Director) received an undisclosed amount for speaking engagements from this organization and his fee is lost somewhere in the 13.5 million dollar conference expense-line according to IRS records.

Family Federation for World Peace
Another Moon organization which held a meeting in Washington in 1996. Among the speakers at this event were Beverly LaHaye and Ralph Reed. Over 1500 notables from around the world attended.

National Religious Broadcasters
Members include Pat Robertson, Jerry Falwell, Jimmy Swaggart, Tim LaHaye, Billy Graham, Bill Bright and many others clearly associated with Moon.

Pat Robertson in the early 80s, as Oliver North was trading guns and ammo (and who knows what else) in Nicaragua, was coordinating efforts to use "Operation Blessing" to help supply goods to the Contras. Allegedly these goods included hard cash and gasoline for Contra vehicles.

The head of Operation Blessing was Captain Robert Warren, who was also formerly associated with a CIA group called "Operation Phoenix." Allegedly this was an assassination group that operated in Vietnam. Also associated with this group was... surprise, Oliver North.

The Washington Times Foundation
A pro-Bush Inaugural luncheon, held in Washington D.C. was sponsored by the Washington Times Foundation, another Moon founded group. Among the attendees were Paul Crouch, founder of Trinity Broadcast Network, Robert Schuller, Kenneth Copeland, Jerry Falwell, Don Argue, past president of the National Association of Evangelicals, Pat Boone, a former T.B.N. board member, Billy McCormack (who was a Christian Coalition board member who actually presented Moon with an award) and Southern Baptist Convention President James Merritt.

Council of 56 of the Religious Roundtable
Another Moon associated group is called the 'Council of 56 of the Religious Roundtable'. This group is made up of many of the same members from Rev. Moons' CNP and CRF organizations. It marries leading Moon associated evangelicals to the CIA, the Council for Foreign relations, the Trilateral Commission and Freemasonry. CFR, and TLC are closely tied to the Bilderberg group.

Others with ties are: Jason Russell, Laren Poole, Ben Keesey, Ben Thomson, Adam Finck, James A. Pearson, and Jared White.   All part of a group known as Invisible Children which is staffed almost exclusively with young, 'Christian activists' and could very well have support links to other Christian evangelist organizations,

One can also add in Ralph Reed, former director of the Christian Coalition and member of the conservative think-tank "Heritage Foundation, Dr. James Dobson, Pediatrician, author and publisher, head of Focus On The Family, a Christ-centric organization and magazine, Phyllis Schlafly, and Jay Sekulow, Christian political activist and attorney involved in family values issues from abortion to parents rights.

The Round Table itself lists:

Principles:
Members of the board of directors of the Roundtable were: Ed McAteer, founder and Pres; Jack Stewart, Vice Pres; Bob Amis, M.D.; John Beckett, Intercessors of America; Othal E. Brand; T. Cullen Davis; Nancy DeMoss; Rev. Del Fehsenfeld, Jr., LifeAction Ministries; Dr. E.V. Hill, pastor at Mt. Zion Baptist Church; Rev. Richard Hogue, Nelson Bunker Hunt, Dr. D. James Kennedy, Coral Ridge Presbyterian Church; J.P. Mills; Dr. Paige Patterson, Criswell Center for Biblical Studies; Rev. James Robison, James Robison Evangelistic Association; D.G. Seago, Jr., Mid-Continent, Inc; and Dr. Charles F. Stanley, First Baptist Church of Atlanta.(2,11) In 1986, Dr. James Robison was Vice President and John Beckett was secretary/treasurer.(14) Former Michigan Congressman Mark Siljander has served on the Roundtable board.

Past members of the Council of 56 include:
Jack Amis, M.D.; Ben Armstrong, executive director of National Religious Broadcasters; Rev. Raymond W. Barber, Worth Baptist Church; John Beckett,Intercessors of America; Dr. George Benson, President emeritus of Harding College; Morton Blackwell, President of the Leadership Institute; Neal Blair, President of Free the Eagle; Tim Bobbit; Dick Bott, President of Bott Broadcasting; Dave Breese, President of Christian Destiny; Paul Broadhead; William Bronson; Rev. Fletcher Brothers, Gates Community Chapel; Judy Brown, American Life League; Dr. Roland Byrd; Dr. David E. Calvin, West Ridge Baptist Church; Clay Claiborne, executive director of the Black Silent Majority; Dr. E.M. Cohron; Dale Collins; W.A. Criswell, Criswell Center for Biblical Studies; Paul Crouch, President of Trinity Broadcasting Network; Mary Crowley; Dr. Paul Cunningham, pastor of Nazarene College Church; Dick Dingman, Republican Study Commission; Dr. Jerry

Falwell, Moral Majority, Old Time Gospel Hour and Thomas Road Baptist Church; Rev. Charles Firoe, John Fisher, American Security Council; Charles Fitzgerald, director of Operation Lifeline; Ken Fonas, the Fonas Corporation; Richard Ford, Coordinated Consulting; Rev. Roger Fulton, Neighborhood Church of New York; Peter B. Gamma, Jr., National Pro-Life PAC; Ellen Garwood; General Daniel Graham, President of High Frontier; R.M.Goddard; Robert Grant, Christian Voice; Lloyd Hansen; Dr. Roy Harthern, Calvary Assembly; Richard Headrick; Senator Jesse Helms(R-NC); Steve Herring; Rev. Melvin Hodges, 1st Baptist Church of Glen Oakes; Don Howard, Accelerated Christian Education; Mildred Faye Jefferson, M.D.; Congressman James Jeffries; Representative Louis (Woody) Jenkins, Friends of the Americas; George B. Jones; Dan S. Kauffman; General George Keegan, Jr.; James Kennedy, pastor of Coral Ridge Presbyterian Church; Bill Keyes, Black PAC; General Albion Knight, Jr.; Beverly LaHaye, President Concerned Women for America; Dr. Tim LaHaye, Scott Memorial Baptist Church; Reed Larson, President of Right to Work; Larry Lea, pastor of Church on the Rock; Marian Maddox, Point of View Radio; Connie Marshner, President of the Family Coalition; Don McAlvany, President of the International Collectors Associates; Bob McCustion, chairman of Faith Ministries; Dr. William H. Marshner, chairman of the Department of Theology at Christendom College; Congressman Larry McDonald (deceased); Jay Menefee, Robert Metcalf; Dr. Bobby Moore, Broadway Baptist Church; Dr. Gary North, Christian Economics Foundation; Larry Parish; Paige Patterson, President of the Criswell Institute; Howard Phillips, The Conservative Caucus; Dr. William A. Powell, Sr., Editor of the Southern Baptist Journal; Randall R. Rader, deputy counsel to the Senate Subcommittee on the Constitution; Dr. Ross Rhoads, Calvary Presbyterian Church; Bill Richardson, California State Senate; Bobby Richardson, Ben LippenSchool; Gary Richardson; Rev. Tom Riner; Phyllis Schlafly, President of the Eagle Forum; Earl Seall, White's Ferry Road Church of Christ; Cory SerVaas, editor and publisher of the Saturday Evening Post; Doug Shadoux, National Republican Party; William S.Smith; Scott Stanley, editor of Conservative Digest; Rev. George Swanson; Helen Marie Taylor, U.S. Representative to the United Nations; William Taylor; Bob Tilton, Bob Tilton Television Ministry; Michael Valerio; Bob Weiner, President of Maranatha Ministries; Paul Weyrich, President of the Free Congress Foundation; Earl E. Whitwell, Kim Wickes, Kim's Ministries; Don Wildmon, President of the National Federation for Decency; Rev.John Wilkerson, Bethel Temple; Rev. Ralph Wilkerson, Melodyland Church, J.C. Willke, M.D., President of National Right to Life, and Jack Wilson, executive director of the Council for National Policy.(2,12).

The following are a few shortened bios from the same source, associated with this Roundtable of 56...

Govt Connections:
Major General George J. Keegan, Jr. was the chief of the U.S. Air Defense Intelligence and member of the Joint Chiefs of Staff, worked for the CIA from 1963-1966
General Daniel Graham (ret.) During the Vietnam war from1967-1968 he was chief of the Army's military intelligence estimates. In 1971 Graham served as director of collections for the Defense Intelligence Agency, the pentagon's version of the CIA. In 1973 Graham

served as a deputy to CIA Director William Colby and from 1974-1976 he was the director of the Defense Intelligence Agency

Groups belonging to the Roundtable include:
The Christian Broadcasting Network, Billy Graham Evangelistic Association, Moral Majority, Christian Voice,Church League of America, National Religious Broadcasters, Campus Crusade for Christ, Plymouth Rock Foundation, National Association of Evangelicals, Gideon Bible, Wycliffe Bible Associates, and Intercessors for America.(15) Ed McAteer was sales marketing manager for Colgate-Palmolive Company when he retired to become the national field director of the Christian Freedom Foundation (CFF), and organization devoted to training evangelicals for places of leadership in government. From there McAteer moved to the righting Conservative Caucus where he served as national field director until founding the Religious Roundtable.(1) He is or was a member of the board of the evangelical Wycliffe Bible Associates.

Franklin Graham's (son of world renowned evangelist Rev. Billy Graham, and heir to the very lucrative and influential Billy Graham Evangelistic Ministries) answer to a question by NBC's Tom Brokaw, ..."it's very important that all the faiths, all the denominations are coming together, cooperating together, working together; it is a wonderful testimony to the spirit of America, and the dedication of the American people."

So if the first listing of those in the CFR read like a who's who in Banking and Business then this list ought to read like a who's who for the Evangelical Community. This is one reason I see the Evangelical control of the GOP as one of the worst dangers facing We the People today in America who want to stand up for our Constitution.

First off, the history of the world shows that any time you have Religion and Politics mixed you usually end up with persecution in one form or another. One simply has to go back to the Dark Ages with the influence in Government the RCC had to get a clear picture of what's involved when the Church has political power.

But the worst thing if I was going to resort to using the Bible is that this was all for told by the very Apostles and even in the Book of Revelations that so many Evangelical's have written about. It, from at least a Biblical perspective is nothing short of the rise of the Great Whore of Babylon. But, I can also remember the day and time when many Evangelicals once considered the Roman Catholic Church the great Whore simply because of its roots in ancient Pagan idealism with Saint Worship, Mary elevated to Mother of God status, etc. If what many Evangelicals once thought was true, then in reality the illegitimate child of that Whore has come home to roost.

If you have not noticed by now I am somewhat anti-religious when it comes to one group of so-called Christians having religious control of a party, wanting to make sure everyone lives up to their standard, putting their idea of what it means to be Christian above every other Christian in this country, acting as if all American's should only have one faith even though this country was founded upon religious liberty, and in general reminding me more and more why these type of Religious Zealots have always been dangerous down through history: Middle Ages acts of the Catholic Church, Salem Witch Trials, you name it on up to another version of religious hate in the form of what happened on 911. Religion and Politics blended together has never once in World History brought anything in the end run but ruin. By the way, to all of you who are Presbyterian, Catholic, Mormon, Unitarian, United Methodist, etc for the most part Evangelical Fundamentalism in American considers you apostate. They may speak your language but in reality they are not your friend.

They consider themselves above other Christians in this country, they give lip service to helping the community, but in general they do little to actually help society. They want nothing less than every child in America indoctrinated in their idea of the Gospel, of Doctrine, and of Science. Why do you think they hate Public Education in general? You cannot brain wash someone in more Liberal education even if it is true the Liberals tend to run higher education. That is because liberal secular education teaches you to think and search the facts. Fundamentalists only rely upon cramming what they want you to know down your throats and God help you if you disagree.

Even though every ounce of scientifically derived evidence supports an old universe and a several billion year old earth these guys want the public schools to teach a literal seven day Creation dating back about 6000 years at most. They have no real scientific research to back up anything, they practice their own version of intellectualism, they helped spawn the Gospel of Prosperity, their idealisms give rise to fanatics who shoot abortion Doctors, and guys like that Pastor a bit back using Bill Boards telling everyone the world was going to end. Listen to them daily on the radio and here what they think about us more Liberal Christians, about people of other faiths and that alone will tell you what they would do if they had total control of politics.

Basically I hate all forms of religious self righteousness that thinks it is above everyone else no matter what the background faith such a system arises from. I support their right to believe as they desire. But I do not support them telling us we have to see things the way they see things. To me they are no better than the Zealots of the Arab extreme out there wanting to kill all Americans in the name of their God.

I support religious freedom as did the Founding Father's of this Country many of whom had different beliefs from the modern day Fundamentalists. Yes, I hate bigotry of any type no matter what name it comes in, even the name of God or in the name of Atheistic idealism. There is nothing un-American about prayer, about moral values, about the value of life, about believing in God no matter what name one calls the Creator by. But it is un-American to want everyone to conform to your brand of religion whither you name the name of Christ or Allah or yourself. That is exactly the type of religious bigotry our founding Fathers wrote language to protect us from.

Many of our Founding Fathers prayed. Washington prayed before each battle and saw the hand of God in every step along the way. Others saw God in what they termed divine providence.

Yes, it is not freedom from Religion, but Freedom of Religion. But Freedom of Religion is not real Freedom unless it supports all religions including the many brands of the Christian one, including those who worship Allah, those who worship Buddha, those who worship nature and any other religion one can name. Yes, even those who worship no God have a right under our system of Government to believe that way. That is the heart and soul of America and what it means to be an American. The Words say One Nation under God. But it does not anywhere say or proscribe who or what that God is. Nor is the rights of one belief system to be valued over another to the point that no one can pray.

But the connection between the CFR, the Rev. Moon's funding of major evangelical groups, and the Gospel of Love being turned into anything but Love really opens up a new avenue of discovery on what is going on in America with the Christian, or at least, so-called Christian Church.

Basically, when you look at the work and pattern of the CFR towards a One World Government and their encroachment into the heart of what at least claims to be the Body of Christ on earth if I was going to begin to quote scripture I'd probably start with the verse that says in the Last Days they will have a form of Godliness, but deny the power there in. I'd also move on to those verses that speak of a falling away and how many seeing themselves wise will become the Blind leading the blind. From there I'd go on to the Book of Revelation and show how the One World Government goes hand in hand with the rise of the one world religion: that Great Whore of Babylon and how everything minus one key element seems to be setting the Church up to become at least part of that killer of the Saints.

It is not that I am against an eventual democratic coming together of the Nations of the World. I am also not against better understanding and dialog between the different faiths. But the CFR's goals are anything but a democratic world Government and there should given the foundation of our Constitution be absolutely no acceptance by the religious community of those goals.   Yet, here we have today some of the major leaders in the Evangelical Community along with many of their major outreach organizations not only receiving funds directly and indirectly from the CFR through its agents, but also in many cases joining that organization. To put this as blunt as I can in terms most evangelicals can understand: A House divided cannot stand. Even more blunt: Accepting money from the Devil comes with bondage.

But that raises an even more vital question in my mind. Are they actually a House divided?

The Roman Empire at the time Christianity became the official State Religion of the Roman Empire had many other religions operating at the same time. But the one that had the most followers was those who worshiped the god Mithras. The period of that worship was from the 1st to 4th centuries AD. Information on the cult is based mainly on interpretations of the many surviving monuments. The most characteristic of these are depictions of Mithras as being born from a rock, and as sacrificing a bull.

"Early Christianity ... in general, resembles Mithraism in a number of respects enough to make Christian apologists scramble to invent creative theological explanations to account for the similarities. The central celebrations of Roman Catholics very much resembles the holiday feasts of Mithraism. (see: Meyer, Marvin (2006). "The Mithras Liturgy". In A.J. Levine, Dale C. Allison, Jr., and John Dominic Crossan. The historical Jesus in context. New Jersey. pp. 179. ISBN 0-691-00991-0. Retrieved 2011-01-20.)

Though not much is known about the full practice and beliefs of this religion it can be argued by indirect evidence that this pagan religion both influenced those of the Council of Nicaea and was perhaps the first Pagan religion to find its ideas incorporated into the Church.

The Catholic Encyclopedia as well as the early Church Fathers found this religion of Mithras very disturbing, as there are so many similarities between the two religions, as follows:

1) Hundreds of years before Jesus, according to the Mithraic religion, three Wise Men of Persia came to visit the baby savior-god Mithra, bring him gifts of gold, myrrh and frankincense.

2) Mithra was born on December 25 as told in the "Great Religions of the World", page 330; "…it was the winter solstice celebrated by ancients as the birthday of Mithraism's sun god".

3) According to Mithraism, before Mithra died on a cross, he celebrated a "Last Supper with his twelve disciples, who represented the twelve signs of the zodiac.

4) After the death of Mithra, his body was laid to rest in a rock tomb.

5) Mithra had a celibate priesthood. Highest Position was titled Father.

6) Mithra ascended into heaven during the spring (Passover) equinox (the time when the sun crosses the equator making night and day of equal length).

7.) Even predating this in the area of UR where Abraham eventually immigrated out of their Goddess Inanna has a similar story told about her.

The pagan Emperor Constantine, who believed in the sun god, Mithras, designated a certain day of the week to him, Sunday, which means, "the day of the sun."   He is also the Ruler who during a time of near civil war between Christians and Pagans called the

Council together, presided over it having last say on what it adopted as beliefs, etc, and Declared himself a Christian after the Council established all they did. It is interesting to note that his family had befriended not the majority of Christians(The ones who became known as Trinitarians), but those who where Arian in their belief. On his death bed, when he was finally baptized it was one of the Arian Priests who performed the ceremony even though officially the Catholic Church he founded considered them apostate.

Basically, Constantine just prior to the Council he called had faced a Roman Empire on the brink of civil war with the Christian's and the Pagan's fighting each other. When you look at how little in the end run Constantine actually accepted the teachings of this New World Religion one see's his real desire was unity even if that required establishing one central religion to replace all the other religions Rome had once worshipped. This issue when you consider he ruled over that Council tends to call into question just how guided by God that whole Council of Nicaea. Sure Christianity had been around as a slowly growing, often persecuted Sect or break off out of Judaism since the time of Christ. And, yes, history shows through many who came after Christ and the Apostles that many letters, which many claimed where authored by the Disciples, where in existence. But the discourse and written arguments that existed within the Church since at least the first Century after the Fall of Jerusalem show the view points within different branches where anything but unitary.

In fact, about 100 years prior to this Council there had existed a viewpoint on the very Nature of God that was contrary to the later developed Trinity view. A Priest by the name of Sibelius had promoted something very different about the nature of Christ, the Son of God and the Father. He saw not three Persons being one God. He saw one Person the Father manifested in different modes. God in the Old Testament Times was the Father, who later became the Son, who after the Resurrection was further manifested as the Spirit. At one point, if numbers had been considered as translating to Orthodoxy the majority of the Christian world believed and followed this idea. It was not till Tertullian, a one time follower of Sibelius having broke with that group coined the Latin term Persona to explain the nature of God the Father, God the Son, and God the Holy Spirit that the roots of what later became Christian Doctrine began. But if one looks at the Latin term PERSONA the meaning is actually of a mask an Actor wore on stage. The biggest real difference between Tertullian and the older Modalists idea was that Tertullian saw the different Masks as an eternal part of God's being instead of something temporary. But behind those Masks he still held to their being one individual who is God. That is far closer to Modalism than what later became accepted Church teaching. By that time persona had evolved into what we today think of as personality.

Many Christians in attempts to support their view of inerrant scriptures and doctrine often point out that the closer to the time of Christ one gets the more closer to the teachings of Christ one comes. If I was to follow that logic here I might suggest that at the 3rd century something more like Modalism in one form or another was being taught, not a full developed Trinity Doctrine. I also would point out that Hebrews 1:3 uses the following words about Christ and the Father: "Christ is the expressed or revealed image of God's

Person. The Greek word for Person actually implies the idea of individual. Basically, Christ was the in the flesh revealed image of the individual of the Father. This is far closer to Tertullian's idea than what came later on with or without adding in the Holy Spirit. Yes, it like Tertullian goes beyond the idea of some temporary mode. But it also falls far short of the idea of three individuals being one God.

Pope Leo X, made this curious declaration, "It was well known how profitable this fable of Christ has been to us" ("The Diegesis" by Rev. Robert Taylor, footnote, p. 35). Considering the Pope by Catholic belief and tradition is seen as the VICAR of Christ and the fact that at least this Pope saw Christ as only a fable or fairy tale there seems to be the implication that one can speak for Christ even if one does not believe in Christ at the heart of at least the Catholic established religion. Makes one wonder how many of the early priests at the forming of the established Christian religion saw the story of Christ the same way? Speaks loads to all doctrine and tradition they set forth if that is the case.

Tertullian first coined the term trinitas from which the English word 'trinity' is derived. He clarifies thus the 'mystery of the divine economy... which of the unity makes a trinity, placing the three in order not of quality but of sequence, different not in substance but in aspect, not in power but in manifestation' (qtd. in Lonergan 46). Tertullian did not consider the Father and Son co-eternal: 'There was a time when there was neither sin to make God a judge, nor a son to make God a Father' (qtd. in Lonergan 48); nor did he consider them co-equal: 'For the Father is the whole substance, whereas the Son is something derived from it' (qtd. in Lonergan 48). It was the later Church at the time of Constantine that adopted those two add on's to their doctrine.

These same arguments in different forms reappeared at the Council of Nicaea. Modalism, as taught by Sabellianism, while already condemned, had its thoughts resurface under the presentation of the anti-Arians that later was molded into the Trinity Doctrine. However, it is true that a majority of Christians at this time favored the Eusebius of Nicomedia submitted Arian creed or at least the general idea that Christ was different from God and a man indwelled and empowered by God. A line in a Popular movie about Christian's who at one point believed Christ was a man woke up to a Christian World that now held as doctrine that Christ was both God and man is very true. In reality, it was never that the Trinity Doctrine was the majority view prior to this Council. It was what became the established view because the most powerful Bishops upheld that view. Modalism exists today in a modified format within the United Pentecostal Church and certain Apostolic Pentecostal Churches, etc.

Arian beliefs resurfaced with the Jehovah Witness group and a few others from time to time. But the Trinity doctrine is accepted by the majority of Churches even though its origin has roots more in Greek thought and in Stoic beliefs and was never the real consensus belief prior to the Council of Nicaea led by a man with Pagan roots and leanings towards the Arian view.

In summary, the common culture of the day was one with belief in triune gods. From ancient Sumerian's Anu, Enlil, and Enki and Egypt's dual trinities of Amun-Re-Ptah and Isis, Osiris, and Horus to Rome's Jupiter, Juno, and Minerva the whole concept of paganism revolved around the magic number of three. For the most part in spite of what early Church Fathers had pinned about the subject the established Church incorporated Pagan ideas into their own doctrines. They then not only added on to the basic one's, but used them as a guide in later establishing what was Scripture or Cannon and what was not.

While one is free to draw your own conclusions and it is true one cannot prove that Christianity is Paganism recoated. There is a lot of Historical evidence that points to at least Pagan belief admixture into established Christian doctrine and belief. To me it makes the whole subject suspect and calls into question every doctrine of the Church and the Bible as far as the New Testament goes. In short, if the Catholic Church is the Whore of Babylon I'd tend to see the rest of Christianity as the illegitimate off spring of that same Whore of Babylon. It is also interesting that the Book of Revelations likens the Spiritual Whore of Babylon as the Mother of all Harlots. In essence, at least from an historical perspective the Whore did have offspring even if those offspring where born under division and strife.

The term Whore or one who prostitutes oneself rather fit's the early Church. In essence, by joining with Constantine the Church aligned itself with all the pomp and power of the Roman Empire. Instead of being those who where persecuted, they would have the protection of the State and the ability to turn tables on the Pagans themselves.

In essence they took on all the corruption of the State, lost their position as "pure bride of Christ", exchanged a simple belief in God and Christ for another sort of belief based upon traditions of men and the added in ideas of pagan belief. In short, they became a whore for power, protection, and money. They started to match up to the verse in the Bible that says in the last days they will have a form of godliness, but deny the power within.

So in reality it is not a far leap to see them once again taking on the corruption of the State or World system according to Christ that belongs to the Devil. Their roots have more ties to the world system of politics than perhaps to the honest Gospel of Christ.

More on Person of Christ

Ignatius in the Epistle to the Magnesians 8.2 regarded God as an undifferentiated monad in His essential being, the Son and the Spirit being merely forms of modes of the Father's self-revelation, only distinguishable from Him in the process of revelation. He placed much emphasis upon the Gospel of John and how Christ was God's word or spoken idea. To this early Church at his time it is God who has revealed Himself in His Son Jesus Christ, the distinction being at the moment of Incarnation and thus ending at the Ascension. So here even before Tertullian's time there is no mention of eternal Sonship. This was back in 98 and 117 AD. Following the logic that they where closer to Christ's time and less influenced by later Pagan ideas this concept of God and Christ is far different from the later one adopted by the Catholic Church. But it is again reflected in Tertullian's view.

In his work Against Praxeas, Tertullian argues, "Flesh does not become spirit nor spirit flesh. Evidently they can be in one. Of these Jesus is composed, of flesh as man and of spirit as God…" In both cases the later idea that prevailed with the established Church on two natures in one person when it came to Christ rather is reechoed way back. Though in Tertullian we find a sort of pseudo-Arian idea where as flesh he was man and as spirit he was God. This rather calls into question the whole argument between the Arians and what became established Church doctrine on this subject. But the central idea of two natures in one person is present even then.

Clement of Rome (A.D. 95), wrote Brothers, we ought so to think of Jesus Christ, as of God, as "Judge of the living and the dead. So the idea of the divinity of Christ seems to have sound roots all the way back to the time of Christ. Its more the relationship of his two natures and the later developing doctrine of the Trinity that seem to stem from external pagan thought and Greek idealism.

In the Movie De Vinci Code an old idea is presented about Christ having a wife and an offspring. This idea has from time to time surfaced. The problem is it is grounded upon little historical evidence of any type. As a man Christ could have had a relationship with a women. The lack of its mention in either the New Testament writings or later Church father's writings tends to speak volumes on the subject. It does not either way change the original teachings the early Church upheld.

So what we have at least on these two main doctrines is that there is one God, the Father who has revealed himself through His Word that became flesh and as the Son of God by birth is both man as flesh and God as Spirit. That would seem to be the actual early Church belief before Pagan idealism and thought was added in. It is a Doctrine neither Arian nor Trinitarian and more one that took at face value Christ's own words on God and himself. It rather fits well with Hebrews 1:3, "Christ is the expressed image of God's person." Basically taking the term EXPRESSED this goes with the Gospel of John seeing Christ as the Pre-existent Word or outward expression of God. One being or individual who is God, who exists as Spirit and who's Spirit brought forth a Son both God and man in one person. The eternal Word of God as spirit and the fleshly Son of God by birth. Close to what later became Christian Doctrine. But it lacks the Pagan aspects that the later Trinity Doctrine encompassed.

My point in all this is that there are grounds to question if what calls itself the Church today is actually the real Body of Christ or just some admixture of Paganism and Christian thought and practice. When I listen to many of the so-called Preacher's out there today I hear very little of the simply faith Christ offered and far more of an preaching of their own words and the mind of modern man. They tend to remind me of a line in the movie "Oh, God" where George Burns, playing God, tells John Denver to go tell God's Quarterback to quit preaching his words, since he quit preaching mine long ago. Basically, what one finds in different forms in the Evangelical message today is a Prosperity Gospel, a Gospel that claims to represent the love of Christ all the while preaching hatred and intolerance towards anyone different from them as often displayed in the words and attitudes they have towards Gays and towards those of the Islamic faith. This all runs in total contrast to Christ who in every case told the rich to give away everything they have, told those who where attacked because of their faith to turn the other cheek, told his followers to walk in love, and who's later disciples spoke often of the fruits of the Spirit (Love, Joy, Peace) as the hallmark of a real life touched by Christ.

These so-called modern Christians not only display in the words and deeds little of those fruits of the Spirit, they are in a lot of cases when it comes to their religious leaders heaping up more treasures on earth than those in Heaven. They are also the first to be totally against anything to do with the Government helping the poor. And yet, in many cases they do little themselves to aid those in need except in the case of major events when one could argue they all seem to come out of the wood work when the media is involved. When I listen to their words and notice their actions I am reminded of those religious leaders Christ spoke about doing long winded prayers in public places to draw attention to themselves. In many ways the Modern Church fails to live up to not only the words of Christ, but, also, the example the Apostle's gave in the Bible which they in general claim as the Inerrant Word of God and foundation of all faith and practice.

Even in the area of Politics they fall short. The only thing Christ ever said about the political arena was to give unto Caesar what is Caesar's. Christ never once even in the presence of a Roman leader implied that his Kingdom, or the Kingdom of those who would follow him was of this earth. The Testimony of the entire Bible is that the world and the political system belongs to the Devil. And yet, going back to those earlier mentioned laws that run contrary to the Constitution that almost all Christian's claim is founded upon Biblical Principles one can note how many of those who claim the name of Christ voted for laws that violate that very document.

The common idea they refer to is being the salt of the earth. The problem is every passage that term comes from spoke about their lives and not how they vote in some election. Salt of the earth is about the way you're life provides a testimony to the world. Not about how you vote in some election. Sure, I support voting you're conscience. That's the whole idea behind our form of Government. But, what you believe cannot be used as a tool to force others into the Kingdom of Heaven. Nor does the belief of anyone religion belong being via political power forced upon everyone else till the point you trample upon their rights if one is going to be honest to the Constitution.

So many Christian's today, at least those in the Evangelical Fundamentalists line think the World hates them and is out to get them. In reality what the vast majority of us hate has nothing to do with Christ. It is the attitude most of those in that religious line have towards everyone else. That life that is supposed to be a testimony to Christ has become nothing but a mockery of Him in the eyes of a majority of people in this Country. Even most Atheist if asked what a Christian is supposed to live like would say you display little of that type of life when it comes to how you speak and deal with others. Sure you could argue they are against you anyway. But, the thing is when you look at the example of Christ, when you look at the example of the Apostles they are correct. If you're life speaks far more than you're words, which are bad enough, then you have no part in the real Kingdom of Heaven.

Adding to this how quickly you have sold you're principles out to an organization that runs so contrary to those same Biblical Principles you say under lines our Constitution I cannot see where the Church is anything more today than a sell out to the system it warned us about long ago.

The Oklohoma City Bombing was the worst case of domestic terrorism commited in America to date. But it might have been more than a domestic case. The 1993 WTC bombing materials had been purchased with the credit card of a US Muslim and an FBI provocateur named Melvin Lattimore. Melvin Lattimore was seen by 4 witnesses in McVeigh's car at the OKC Travelers Aid office adjacent to the Murrah federal building just ONE DAY before the OKC bombing. Six FBI agents spent 9 months browbeating the 4 witnesses, trying to make them change their story about seeing Lattimore at the Travelers Aid. Lattimore was the roommate of the 20th 9/11 hijacker Zacarias Moussaoui while he attended the Airman flight school in Norman Oklahoma in 2000 and 2001. Lattimore was also the roomate of 9/11 hijackers Al Hazmi and Al Shehhi in Norman Oklahoma. Retired Air Force General Benton K. Partin informed AG Ashcroft in August 2001 of the Travelers Aid story in writing and in person. Yet, not surprisingly, nothing was done by Ashcroft about Lattimore.

Jane Graham worked for HUD on the seventh floor of the federal building. While viewing a video tape of the original television coverage of the bombing, she noticed men who she had seen in the building the day before and again on the morning of the bombing. They were dressed like the building's maintenance workers, but she had never seen them before. On the morning of the bombing at approximately 8:00 a.m. "these two men were coming out of the stairwell on the first floor. Both were dressed in blue pants and shirts like our maintenance workers. They walked by me and I thought at the time they looked so different from our normal people that are employed in our building."
Jane saw three different men in the parking garage beneath the Murrah building who had what she thought was telephone wiring and a block of solid putty-colored substance. They had plans of the building they were discussing or arguing. Apparently, there was a disagreement because one of the men was pointing to various areas in the garage. They

were talking about the plans of the building. "I assumed they were telephone workers. When they saw me watching them, they took this wiring and whatever else was in their hands and put it into a paper sack, behind the passenger's seat in a...faded green station wagon."

Jane's office was on the seventh floor, but she had just gone to the ninth when the blast occurred. "In reflecting on this I want to specify that the first bomb, the first impact was a waving effect, like an earthquake, which lasted several seconds. About six or seven seconds later a bomb exploded; there was an entirely different sound and thrust. It was like it came right from the center up, we could feel the floor move. The last thing I remember was looking up and seeing the roof being blown off."

Terrance Yeakey, an Oklahoma City police officer was one of the first to arrive at the scene of the bombing. His observations of federal agents' actions there, his direct interactions with his superiors about the "operation gone wrong", and his access to documentation dealing with the bombing, led him to make the following statement .
"My guess is the more time an officer has to think about the screw-up, the more he is going to question what happened.... Can you imagine what would be coming down now if that had been our officers who had let this happen? Because it was the feds that did this and not the locals, is the reason it's okay. The sad truth of the matter is that they have so many police officers convinced that by covering up the truth about the operation gone wrong that they are actually doing our citizens a favor. What I want to know is how many other operations have they had that blew up in their faces? Makes you stop and take another look at Waco."

The following are excerpts from an Oklahoma City policeman's letter to a bombing victim whom he had befriended. Officer Terrance Yeakey was one of the first rescuers at the scene of the bombing. As the letter indicates, he saw many disturbing things and much evidence that is contradictory to the OFFICIAL VERSION of the story.

The letter begins,"The man that you and I were talking about in the pictures, I have made the mistake of asking too many questions as to his role in the bombing, and was told to back off. I was told by several officers he was an ATF agent who was overseeing the bombing plot and at the time the photos were taken he was calling in his report of what had just went down! Luke Franey (ATF agent who said he was in the building at the time of the explosion) was not in the building at the time of the blast. I know this for a fact. I saw him! I also saw full riot gear worn, with rifles in hand, why?"

"Knowing what I know now, and understanding fully just what went down that morning, makes me ashamed to wear a badge from Oklahoma City's Police Department. I took an oath to uphold the Law and to enforce the Law to the best of my ability. This is something I cannot honestly do if I keep my silence as I am ordered to do."

"My guess is, the more time an officer has to think about the screw up, the more he is going to question what happened. Can you imagine what would be coming down now if that had been our officers who had let this happen? Because it was the feds that did this and not the locals, is the reason it's okay. If I tried to explain it to you the way it was explained to me, and the ridiculous reason for having our own police departments falsify their reports to their fellow officers, to the citizens of the city and to our country, you would understand why I feel the way I do about all this."

"I truly believe there are other officers like me out there who would not settle for anything but the truth; it is just a matter of finding them. The only true problem as I see it is, who do we turn to then? I believe that a lot of the problems the officers are having right now are because some of them know what really happened and can't deal with it, and others like myself made the mistake of trusting the one person we were supposed to be able to turn to (the chaplain) only to be stabbed in the back."

"I would consider it to be an insult to my profession as a police officer and to the citizens of Oklahoma for ANY of the City, State or Federal agents that stood by and let this happen, to be recognized as anything other than their part in participation in letting this happen. For those who ran from the scene to change their attire to hide the fact that they were there, should be judged as cowards."

"You were right all along and I am truly sorry I doubted you and your motives about recording history. Everyone was behind you until you started asking questions as I did, as to how so many federal agents arrived at the scene at the same time. I worry about you and your young family because of some of the statements that have been made towards me, a police officer! I am not worried for myself, but for you and your group. I would not be afraid to say at this time that you and your family could be harmed if you get any closer to the truth. At this time I think for your well-being it is best for you to distance yourself and others from those of us who have stirred up too many questions about the altering and falsifying of the federal investigation's reports. Altering and falsifying of the federal investigation's reports."

"It is vital that people like you, Edye Smith and others keep asking questions and demanding answers for the actions of our federal government and law enforcement agencies that knew beforehand and participated in the cover-up. Don't make the mistake as I did and ask the wrong people."

"If our history books and records are ever truly corrected about that day, it will show this and maybe even some lame excuse as to why it happened, but I truly don't believe it will from what I now know to be the truth. I am sad to say that I believe my days as a police officer are numbered because of all of this."

Tragically, just two days before he was to be awarded the Medal of Valor for his efforts in the rescue effort, he was found dead. The OFFICIAL VERSION called his death "suicide". The following facts in the case tell a different story:

"He kept telling me it wasn't what I thought it was," said his ex-wife, Tonia Rivera. The story of the reluctant hero was nothing more than a 'thin veil of truth' which covered up a 'mountain of deceit.' There came a time about mid-year where they were forcing him into going to these award ceremonies; as in, 'Yes, you could not go, but we'll make your life hell.' 'I'm no hero,' he would say. 'Nobody that had anything to do with helping those people in that bombing are heroes."

"Shortly after the bombing, Yeakey appeared at his ex-wife's. 'About two weeks before his death he came to my apartment trying to give me these insurance policies,' said Rivera. 'He sat on my living room couch and cried and told me how he had a fight with [his supervisors] Lt. Randall and Maj. Upchurch. He did not tell me what that entailed, but he was scared. He was crying so badly, he was shaking.

"'He wouldn't totally voice whatever it was,' recalled Rivera. 'It was like he'd be just about to tell me he'd want to spill his guts - and then he stopped, and he just cried. And that's when he kept insisting that I take the insurance policy. Why would a guy tell you to take a life insurance policy, knowing it wouldn't pay for a suicide? He obviously knew he was in danger.'

At 9:00 a.m., May 8, 1996, Officer Yeakey was seen exiting his Oklahoma City apartment with nine boxes of videos and files. He then drove to the police station where he had a fight with his supervisors. He was told to 'drop it' or he'd 'wind up dead.' Driving straight to a storage locker he maintained in Kingfisher, he secured his files. What were in the files? According to one of Rivera's sources, incriminating photos and videos of the bombed-out building. Perhaps more.

"While it is not known exactly what transpired next, at approximately 6:00 p.m. that evening, Deputy Sheriff Mike Ramsey noticed an abandoned vehicle in a field. 'Immediately hair stood up on the back of my neck,' said the deputy. Ramsey came upon the empty car which he immediately recognized as Yeakey's. There was blood on both seats and a razor blade lying on the dash. Yeakey was nowhere to be found.

"The deputy immediately called for a homicide investigator, and taped off the scene. Police dogs located Yeakey's body in a ditch, a mile and a half away.

"Dr. Larry Balding, Oklahoma City's Chief Medical Examiner, quickly ruled the death a 'suicide.' Apparently Yeakey had tried to cut himself in the wrists, neck and throat, then after losing approximately two pints of blood, got out of his car, walked a mile and a half over rough terrain, crawled under a barbed wire fence, waded through a culvert, then lay down in a ditch and shot himself in the head.The Oklahoma City Medical Examiner's report described numerous 'superficial' lacerations on the wrists, arms, throat and neck, and a single bullet wound to the right temple.

"The report also showed another curious thing. The bullet had entered just above and in front of the right ear, and had exited towards the bottom of the left ear. Apparently, whoever held the gun held it at a downward angle. A person shooting themself would tend to hold the gun at an upward angle.

"Perhaps the most revealing evidence was that the wound did not have a 'stellate,' the tell-tale star shape caused by the dissipating gasses from the gun's muzzle. At the close range of a suicide weapon, such markings would be clearly present. And if this weren't strange enough, Yeakey's diet-related condition would have made him too weak to walk the mile and a half from his car to where his body was found - especially after losing two to three pints of blood.

"Yet while attending a social function, Rivera claims her sister had a chance encounter with the mortician who worked on Yeakey's body. She was discussing the strange inconsistencies of his death with someone at the party, when the mortician, not knowing the woman was Rivera's sister, spoke up. 'That sounds just like a police officer we worked on in Oklahoma City,' he said. When asked if that man happened to be Terrance Yeakey, the mortician 'freaked'.

"When pressed, he told the shocked relative that the dead man's wrists contained rope burns and handcuff marks. A former FBI agent and police officer, the mortician said that Yeakey's lacerations were already sewn up when the body arrived from the medical examiner's office. Dr. Balding's response to this was that the marks were merely 'skin slippage', resulting from the natural decomposition of the body. Apparently those covering up his death had not counted on this particular mortician's testimony.

Failure Analysis Associates, Inc. had a featured disaster article "The Bombing of the Oklahoma City Federal Building: A Failure Analysis" authored by Dr. Eve H. Hinman, a specialist in designing structures for dynamic loads, particularly those caused by explosions, explaining how the Murrah building was taken down by a single ammonium nitrate fuel oil (ANFO) truck bomb. Contrast this with the "Eglin Blast Effects Study" a 56-page report that includes photographs and data from the Eglin Air Force blast tests, as well as extensive technical analysis of those tests which concluded that "the damage at the Murrah Federal Building is not the result of the truck bomb itself, but rather due to other factors such as locally placed charges within the building itself...."

Puzzle Pieces; a Geopolitical Perspective on the Bad Politics that are creating the Fall of America - "Okla City: 2 High-tech blasts, BATF, Quick Demolition Hides Evidence" and other articles including: "Alternative Education vs Goals 2000; Outcome-Based Education vs Values," "Eyewitnesses of TWA 800 missile," "Development of New World Order in the U.S.," "Federal Reserve, IRS, Illuminati Conspiracy vs Constitution!," "Gulf War Syndrome, 50,000 Veterans, Biologic, Chemical Weapons," "Media and Mind Control, News Editing, Poll Manipulation, No Free Press," "Ruby Ridge, R. Weaver, Waco, Tank + Flame-thrower + Flammable Tear Gas," and "Social Quakes."   All of these leave a trial that generally leads to not only our current events, but to the events leading up to 911.

The March 20, 1996 issue of Strategic Investment newsletter, a classified Pentagon study confirms that the Oklahoma bombing was caused by more than one bomb. A classified report prepared by two independent Pentagon experts has concluded that the destruction of the federal building in Oklahoma City in April 1995 was caused by five separate bombs. The two experts reached the same conclusion for the same technical reasons.

Freedom Network News at the time that seismograph readouts at the University of Oklahoma indicated more than one blast impulse. Independent ordnance experts, including a Navy Commander, unanimously agreed that a car-bomb with low intensity fertilizer explosives could not have inflicted such extensive damage to the building and that it was highly likely that high-intensity explosives had been wired directly to the columns. Our suspicion then as now is that it was an "inside job." But by whom is the mystery. Strategic Investment reports that the multiple bombings had a Middle Eastern "signature." Others find the whole business to be extremely fishy because of the fact that no ATF or FBI agents were in their offices at the time of the blast [about 9:05 a.m.] — and that evidence pertaining to both Waco and Mena had been stored there.

The remains of the half-destroyed Federal building were demolished just a few weeks after the explosion. "I certainly stand by my remarks, because it's widely known that McVeigh was anti-government. I think that he was a right-winger, and I think the current tea party people, while I'm not saying that they're proposing violence, they're anti-government," party Chairman Wallace Collins said. Timothy McVeigh was not a "Christian terrorist." He was born of Christian parents and lived in a nominally Christian culture, sure, but he did not perpetrate his crime in the name of the Christian God.

In a response filed to a federal judge's order May 11, an FBI official offered no denials about the existence of video images captured by more than 20 surveillance cameras operating prior to 9:02 a.m. on April 19, 1995, in the vicinity of the Alfred P. Murrah Federal Building in downtown Oklahoma City. Instead, he explained that officials at the bureau merely cannot find the tapes and raised the possibility that they "might have been misfiled and thus could be located somewhere other than in the OKBOMB file (though it would be impossible to know where)." The F.B.I. finally released 20 secret, long-held security camera tapes of the deadly 1995 Oklahoma City bombing, after a Freedom of Information Act request from Utah attorney Jesse Trentadue. The disturbing, soundless images don't show the actual bombing of the Alfred P. Murrah Federal Building, on 9:02 a.m. April 19, 1995, but do provide images of the chaos, minutes after the bombing, captured from security tapes of nearby buildings. Long-secret security tapes showing the chaos immediately after the 1995 bombing of the Oklahoma City federal building are blank in the minutes before the blast and appear to have been edited, an attorney who obtained the recordings said Sunday [9/27/2009]. A former deputy assistant director of the FBI with extensive experience in domestic terrorism cases is calling for additional investigation into the 1995 bombing of the A.P. Murrah Federal Building. As one of the world's foremost experts in both the theoretical and practical applications of explosives technology, Brigadier General Benton K. Partin (USAF, retired) possesses virtually unparalleled qualifications to authoritatively evaluate the public-source information available on the bombing.

From the start, the general expressed very strong misgivings about the "official" story —
that the horrendous damage to the federal building had been caused solely by the reported
truck bomb. Too many facts, he said, "simply just don't add up" to support that convenient
explanation.

> Many witnesses who saw bomb squad trucks and personnel around the Murrah
> Building before the blast.
> • The absence of ATF agents from their offices in the Murrah Building at the time
> of the blast.
> • ATF-FBI informant Carol Howe's testimony that she gave specific warning.
> • Federal informant Cary Gagen's testimony (supported by a corroborating
> witness) that he warned authorities on April 6th.
> • A U.S. Marshals' memo of March 22, 1995 warning of expected bomb attacks on
> federal buildings.

Loudenslager was seen by many witnesses, including police officers and rescue workers,
involved in a very "heated" confrontation. Much of his anger being due to the fact that he
felt that the B.A.T.F. and D.E.A. were responsible for the extent of the blast damage.
However to the astonishment of those who had seen him in the immediate aftermath of the
bombing, it was later reported that Loudenslager was found at his desk, a victim of the
9:02 A.M. bombing. To the absolute astonishment of a large number of police officers
and rescue workers, it was later reported that G.S.A. employee Mike Loudenslager's body
had been found inside the Murrah Building the following Sunday, still at his desk, a victim
of the 9:02 A.M. bombing! This, mind you, after he'd already been seen alive and well by
numerous rescue workers at the bomb-site AFTER the bombing! He is also officially listed
as one of the 168 bombing fatalities.

Two key witnesses in the Oklahoma City bombing case never appeared to testify at the
Denver trial of Timothy McVeigh, one of the two accused of being responsible for the
bombing, because they are dead. One death has been labeled a suicide. The other victim
was killed in an air crash. Both deaths took place under questionable circumstances.

Sgt. Yeakey's death was NEVER properly investigated according to the basic standards of
criminal law. Consequently, his death was erroneously ruled a suicide vs. an unsolved
homicide. Yet, in his own words: a number of things about the "bombing" just didn't add
up. If this was a terrorist bombing, then why were police line already up behind the
building when he first arrived, within two minutes after the fact? And where had all of the
ATF & FBI agents come in so quickly outside the building (most relatively unharmed)
when he'd first gotten there as well?

For a few years, Oklahoma State Representative Charles Key, former grand juror Hoppy
Heidelberg, Glenn and Cathy Wilburn, and a great many other Oklahomans called
attention to the many credible eyewitnesses who say they saw Timothy McVeigh with a
man answering the description of John Doe No. 2, or with other men, on the morning of
the Oklahoma City bombing. Also important are the many witnesses who connect

McVeigh and the Ryder truck with other John Does in Kansas. … However, federal prosecutors have pointedly excluded from their list of trial witnesses any of those who have attested to seeing anyone besides McVeigh.

Major Facts:

In April 1995, the Omnibus Counter Terrorism Bill was struggling to get through the US Congress. After the OKC Bombing occurred, the tragedy looked as though it had been tailor-made to rally public support for the tyrannical bill.

The morning of the bombing, the ATF office located inside the Murrah building was empty, unheard of at 9 AM on a weekday.

Oklahoma Congressman Ernest Istook told a victim in a taped conversation in 1995 that the OKC bombing was a failed national security operation that used an FBI provocateur associated with a militia.

The ATF was already putting out a story that the Murrah Building was bombed "because of Waco" only a few hours after the actual blast and before Tim McVeigh was even arrested.

An unexploded bomb was found attached to a gas line inside the building, and a FEMA memo reports at least two additional bombs were found in the Murrah Building. Joe Harp, based on his military explosives experience, identified the additional bombs he saw removed from the building as being military in nature.

General Benton K. Partin, USAF (Ret.) stated in his OKC Bombing report to US Congress that "The bombing of the Alfred P. Murrah Federal Building, Oklahoma City, was not caused solely by the truck bomb. The major factor in its destruction appears to have been detonation of explosives carefully placed at four critical junctures on supporting columns within the building."

Prior to the OKC bombing US Senator Arlan Specter as well as Clinton's NSC director Anthony Lake had been advocating federal national security operations to stop militias in America. Anthony Lake gave a speech to the Council on Foreign Relations (CFR) in the Fall of 1994 in which he said the chief cornerstone of government policy was to "pit our society against militias".

McVeigh was seen with several unidentified individuals, many with middle eastern features in the weeks leading up to the bombing. At the trial, these facts were NOT allowed in as evidence. Also at his trial his sister read a letter from McVeigh to the grand jury in which he told her he was going into the Special Forces Covert Tactical Unit. Survivor Jane Graham tells of three very suspicious men she saw in the Murrah Building Garage the week prior to the bombing, and was shocked by the FBI's obvious disinterest in the matter. Virgil Steele, an elevator inspector at the scene also saw two additional bombs being removed from the building. Reports of additional bombs were confirmed by the OKC fire department. They used trained explosives sniffing dogs to locate those additional bombs, so not only did the devices found in the Murrah Building have to look enough like real bombs to fool the bomb squad, they had to SMELL LIKE REAL EXPLOSIVES TO THE BOMB SNIFFING DOGS.

A Video of Tim McVeigh from a security camera at a McDonald's in Junction City, along with statements from the Ryder employees who rented the truck, can be seen as proof that McVeigh did not rent the Ryder Truck used in the bombing. McVeigh had been filmed by the security camera at the McDonald's just minutes before the time stamped on the rental agreement, wearing clothes that did not match either of the men seen at the truck rental center. The three people interviewed agreed John Does 1 and 2 were dry. Yet to get there he would have had to traveled the mile and a quarter from McDonald's to the rental agency, carless and alone, without getting soaked in the rain.

These are all facts that have been reported by others, that where covered in Press Releases, and that were given in sworn testimony. But all of these facts where ignored along with a connection to Neo-Nazi groups and to certain Arab Extremists. At the very least, if this was some sting operation gone bad as many have suggested the fact our Government came up with a cover story in itself ought to ring alarms in every American's ears, especially to the growing number of citizens out there who distrust our Government to begin with.

Corporatism and Socialism

Historical socialism based upon Marx meant government ownership of the means of production. The Left expected socialism to succeed capitalism, and then, after a brief period, lead to communism under which there would be neither private nor governmental, but rather communal, ownership of property and the means of production. However, history wise both Russia and China's version of such never got beyond the first step which is way some see Socialism as an illusion where its all about power and nothing else.

America's own version of Socialism is a political theory that revolves around substantial government management of the economy. The motivating factor is the desire to improve the lives of the poor. The basic programs they use are welfare, social security, just about all of the social programs the Democratic Party has created over time. The Republican Party doesn't advocate dismantling much of our socialist system, either. Just the portions that tend not to benefit the major corporations that tend to support them. They like protective tariffs and corporate subsidies, their social security reform ideas entail only partial privatization. Classic liberalism (i.e. limited government, free markets and the protection of natural rights) has been the prevailing philosophy in America basically for both Parties even though the Right via the GOP tends to view the Left as Socialists at heart.

If we look at the heart of socialism, commonly termed redistribution of wealth, basically both Parties fail in the aspect of not doing such. The Democrats openly utilize such in most of their tax based programs. But the GOP in its support of Big Corporations and support of tax policies that favor them has not only allowed a lot of what once where American jobs to shift overseas. It has outright in many cases allowed the vast money of those same companies to shift overseas also. It's redistribution of the wealth from America to foreign Nations with their brand. They do this all based upon their open support of the free market system, even though our Founding Fathers who supported the same never intended our free market here to have all the money going to everyone but Americans.

Under the Bush era and the creation of NAFTA even more of our money went out of the Country benefiting in a lot of cases those in Mexico and other countries. At one time Hershey had a large plant out in California which under NAFTA and cheaper wages down in Mexico moved their operation there with the cost of jobs here. There is also a large tax advantage for Corporations to base themselves over seas instead of Stateside. Many in these companies today when asked about the problems back home take an attitude much like those in Apple that it is not their problem to solve America's problems. I would suggest that if our Government did its job as spelled out in the Constitution it would be their problem once a more fair tax system that rewards Companies that stay here more than those that go overseas and hire mostly here over those who do not. This is simply because it all concerns money. Make it cheaper to stay here and the Companies will flock back. Make it cheaper to go overseas and they go where they can make the most money. Plain and simple Economics and nothing more.

Corporatism, implemented by the state, either political Party, or loose organizations like CFR , whether through direct handouts, corporate bailouts, eminent domain, licensing laws, antitrust regulations, or environmental edicts inflicts great harm on the modern American economy. Although leftists often misunderstand the fundamental problem plaguing the economy as being all the fault of Big Banking and Big Cooperation's, they at least recognize its symptoms which many on the right fail to do and often support. However, the Democratic Party itself has fallen prey to this same sort of say one thing and do another. State corporatism is a form of socialism, and it is nearly inevitable in a mixed economy that the introduction of more socialism will cartelize industry and consolidate wealth in the hands of the few. This has always been the history of economics that so many on both sides fail to see. The biggest divide today is the vast difference between the so called 95% and the 1%. But this divide has resulted from Policies and Programs put into place by both Parties that creates State corporatism of one form or another.

Two major political traditions in America offered different views from the very beginning on the proper roles of government. The classical liberals, typified by Thomas Jefferson early on, had their political outlet in the Democratic Party, which, for the most part, stood on the side of limited, constitutional government and individual rights. Those who believed in a strong central government, typified early on by Alexander Hamilton, found their political home first in the Federalist Party, then in the Whig Party, and then in the Republican Party, the last of which openly embraced the doctrine of big government throughout the 19th century though today the situation is somewhat reversed.

Hamilton fought for central banking, high tariffs, and subsidies to corporations to build "internal improvements." Hamilton's first major successor, Henry Clay, called this governmental corporate program the "American System." Which many in the GOP still follow today. The Progressive Era that came later was a time in which both corporatism and socialism received major boosts. The Federal Reserve established a banking oligopoly, guaranteed bailouts for the big bankers, created new barriers to entry for smaller bankers, and was in fact designed by people representing some of the most powerful banking interests in the world, including the National City Bank of New York; Kuhn, Loeb & Company; J.P Morgan Company; and the First National Bank of New York all of which ended up having members in the CFR.

The New Deal and even more the Agricultural Adjustment Administration cartelized the farming industry, and Roosevelt's farm subsidies and price supports have to this day helped to solidify a corporate stronghold in American agriculture which has over time taken it's toll on the family run farm. The New Deal, while a program designed to help the poor in many cases actually ended up helping the Big Corporations via cheap labor under later on added in minimum wage versus Union Labor where the wages where set higher. But I would also be the first to add that Unions have in the past priced their labor out of a job which itself helped send jobs overseas. Unions still perform a vital function to those who work under a Union. But in an ideal situation those Unions need more often to reflect what their local economy can afford. Not every area in this country can afford to pay it's workers top wages. The economics vary from State to State.

In more recent times, Enron was one of the largest lobbying influences behind the international Kyoto Treaty, which would have forced the world to comply with a ghastly web of new regulations much of which are still the agenda of the left via the EPA and would have meant large energy contracts for Enron, had the company not gone bankrupt. The antitrust breakup of Microsoft was a de facto giveaway to competitors such as Netscape while one of the complaints about Microsoft was that it intended merging with AOL, a company with which Netscape has since joined forces.

Bush's farm subsidies and tax cuts are direct welfare for the biggest corporations, and his protectionist trade policies are indirect welfare for politically favored businesses. His recent expansion of Medicare has been both the greatest augmentation of the American welfare state in decades and a giveaway to large pharmaceutical corporations. If universal health care comes to America, the corporations are likely to stay intact but will no longer have to satisfy customers, only the politicians.   In fact, hidden in the whole Obama Care package via the GOP desired mandate was a huge cash flow for the Insurance Agencies. So both Parties in that case through their own versions of politics actually benefited a select few over the majority of American's all in the name of affordable Healthcare.

America doesn't have a free-market economy, and indeed many of the ills associated with free markets are actually the result of state capitalism or socialist corporatism sponsored bit by bit by both sides via members within their ranks from the CFR.   The expansion of government regulations, often done in the name of combating corporate excesses, is frequently supported most enthusiastically by corporate interests.   Sure a lot of the newer EPA stuff is looked down upon. It basically goes to far in its reach for control. But for those out there who have watched the appearance of the Occupy Wall Street movement and have wondered why they hate the system that actually feeds them and gives them what they want part of the problem is they equate the free-market with the system we have at present which is anything but a free market.

The Economic system we have in America today is simply a controlled socialized world market system where excesses related to costs via supply and demand are countered via special interests groups, Government regulations, infusion of cash in the form of special interest tax breaks and bailouts in more recent times, insider trading in the Stock Market, special interest groups under the banner of Citizens United, and bought and sold politicians who themselves control the taxes and the regulations. The Agenda of the CFR has become the actual World Monetary System replacing honest Free Market Economy.

Conservatives, have no difficulty claiming to be the party of freedom in one breath and attacking civil liberties in the next.   Part of this is the influence the Evangelical Right has on the Conservatives in the GOP. Conservatism constantly changes, always adapting itself to provide the minimum amount of freedom that is required to hold together a dominant coalition in the society. Liberalism also adapts to support what it sees as social liberty and freedom. But both do so via control in one form or another of that society. Generally, since society today tends to be consumers they both do so via support of Big Business, Big Banks, etc. This is the heart of the creeping socialism brought about by the CFR. But it is a socialism vastly different from what Marx outlines or even Stalin had ever thought of. It is a socialism where the power is actually in the hands of those who really control the Markets and the Economy. It is an aristocratic domination as with all forms of socialism ever employed. But it hides behind the covering of democracy. The People still get to vote. And their vote does control who get's elected. But all of those running on both sides are already bought and sold by those in the aristocratic domination. Thus, no matter who we elect we keep in one form or another doing the bedding of that aristocratic domination.

At the heart of what has become Conservatism today is the notion that the conservative order is ordained by God and that anyone and anything that opposes the conservative order is infinitely evil. One hears this reflected in speech by people like Rush Limbaugh who has argued at length in the past that Tom Daschle resembles Satan simply because he opposes George Bush's policies. Ever since then, Limbaugh has regularly identified Daschle as "el Diablo". One heard it a lot more recently in ill spoken words by Rush calling a certain women testifying to the Senate on the need for birth control as a Slut and Whore. One also heard it in many of Rick Santorum's own speeches on his views about such and the place of women. The latter even more based upon the notion that their idealism is God ordained.

Conservative strategists construct their messages in a variety of stereotyped ways. One of the most important patterns of conservative message-making is projection. Projection is a psychological notion; it roughly means attacking someone by falsely claiming that they are attacking you. But the Democrats are also guilty of this themselves over and over again. Really, most of the political argument today is more an attempt to see who can beat the other person in this area. Obama, taking a cue from the Occupy Movement has often uttered statements invoking class warfare. But the GOP often walks itself willing into those same arguments by outright ignoring those differences and by using it's twisted rhetoric in attacks upon different groups of its own and the Democrats. In reality, if there was no truth in what the Democrats claim then why not just simply go on about you're business without all the rhetoric? Beating your own drum long enough will just cause people to turn off to what you have to say. Funny thing in all this the real problem: Our Economy is the one thing neither side has honestly addressed.

What calls itself Conservative has actually adopted a psychologically internalized attitude that they are the only one's fit to Govern the people in a way that has tended to actually ignore the Middle Class in favor of the rich and the money they bring to their Party. Crucial to what has become conservatism is the mindset that the people must literally want to be dominated which is why they constantly point out every failure in all the alternatives. They make it so its their way of suffer harm. perfectly overt in the writings of leading conservative theorists such as Burke. Democracy, for them, is not about the mechanisms of voting and office-holding. In fact conservatives hold a wide variety of opinions about such secondary formal matters. For conservatives, rather, democracy is a psychological condition. People who stand by the Constitution, by contrast, believe that they are of equal social worth. Conservatism is the antithesis of democracy. The Democrats are not much better because they rely upon both scare tactics and stronger Government to achieve their power. Basically, both Parties manage the same ends through different means and that end is the people being Dominated in one way or another.

By Burke's own words, social institutions are a kind of capital. A properly ordered society will be blessed with large quantities of this capital. This capital has very particular properties. It is a sprawling tangle of social arrangements and patterns of thought, passed down through generations as part of the culture. It is generally tacit in nature and cannot be rationally analyzed. It is fragile and must be conserved, because a society that lacks it will collapse into anarchy and tyranny. Innovation is bad, therefore, and prejudice is good. Although the institutions can tolerate incremental reforms around the edges, systematic questioning is a threat to social order.

Nothing can be worse for the conservative than rational thought, because when people think rationally they might decide to try replacing inherited institutions with new ones, something that a conservative regards as impossible. This is where the word "conservative" comes from: the supposed importance of conserving established institutions like the Religious Evangelical Right. This is why they fight tooth and nail against abortion, against birth control, against Gay Rights, and against Women's rights, fighting against anything that is based upon ration thinking in favor of tradition. But they ignore the fact that the reason the Constitution took from the Bible the Principles it did about freedom is founded upon doing away with a tradition or conservative thing to begin with. In the New Testament it was the Old World Tradition of the relation between God and Man. In our County's case it was the Conservative Tradition of the King. In each case one finds a more rational replacement of a tradition or in Burke's words a social institutions in favor of something new and evolved which runs so counter to the idealism of Conservatives today.

I will give the Conservatives one key point. The Democrats controlled both parts of Congress during the first 2 years Obama was in office. The Republicans still to this day cannot over ride a veto by the President. And the Democrats still control the Senate. The fiscal downfall belongs back under Bush. But the current inability to work out a stable budget falls back upon the Democrats as long as they have the full say. I do not at all favor the proposed Ryan Budget. Basically, as we get out of war we need to cut back Military spending and focus more on building back America instead of the trillions for the military handout over the next few years. I also take strong difference on that budgets approach to Social Security. But, I will give Ryan his due on at least coming up with a budget as I also give the President his due in proposing one himself.

To the Conservatives the liberals are the American version of the Soviet nomenklatura. They are the Authoritarian Power that must be crushed. But to the Liberals the Conservatives are about the same. The reality is both are. Only the Soviet nomenklatura are actually those behind the public eye pulling the strings.

Basically, for all the name calling every time we have a Liberal in Office we get more influence in our lives via the Government. And every time a Conservative is in control we get more social control on our daily lives. And even more recently more direct assaults upon our Constitution via both parts. This will continue as long as We the People allow it to continue and do not act to recover the Constitutional foundation of our Government.

The problem is to act people must step outside the boundaries of both Parties. To do that one has to first admit that neither Party acts anymore in the best interest of the People. We need a viable third Party in this country populated by men and women willing to ignore the special interest groups with all the money they offer and work as Statesman, instead of puppets under the control of the aristocratic domination. We need to fire all the Bums up in Washington in one clear voice that tells them we have had enough. We need to unite together on a common ground that allows us to be different in our views, our Families National Heritage, our Religious idealism, and at the same time work together for the common good of all the People in keeping with the Constitution just as the framers of that great document did so long ago.

None of that will if worked out translate to a Government of hand outs. It will be a Government as was intended providing a hand up where needed and an atmosphere in our Nation that allows us and our Children to find their own bit of the American Dream. But the central thing is there has to be an awakening of We the People for that type of change to come about.

The end is near a segment of Christians aligned with the religious right think. The global economic meltdown, numerous natural disasters and the threat of radical Islam have fueled a conviction among some evangelicals that these are the last days. But let's suppose for a moment just like in the 30's and 40's which saw similar times that such a state of affairs coupled with the economic and religious mixture of power the CFR has crafted does give rise to another shall we say, version of Hitler given how often we human's never seem to learn from the past. Is there anything we could gain by say looking at the Bible Prophecy and doing a bit of speculation here? Actually, there is a lot we could gain out of those prophecies that given the current world situation, especially in the Middle East does begin to support the idea of a World Leader taking ultimate power.

The books of Daniel, Ezekiel and Revelation foreshadow the arrival of the last days: the growth of strong central governments and the consolidation of independent nations into one superstate led by a seemingly benevolent leader promising world peace. They also give some clues about this coming world leader pointing to not only the region he will come out of, but, also where his ties will be. And today there is a central leadership vacuum both in the CFR and its religious connection and in the Nations of the world that is as ripe for the taking as pre-world war two Germany was. Want proof, look at Greece that just elected Neo-Nazi members into its ruling body and even closer to home look at how many here in this country are fed up with all our present political leaders. So what can we gather about this coming world leader?

1.) He will try to change the laws, perhaps to gain an advantage for his new kingdom and era [Dan 7:25]

2.) He will speak boastfully [Daniel 7:8; Rev 13:5]

3.) He comes from among ten kings in the restored Roman Empire; his authority will have similarities to the ancient Babylonians, Persians, and Greeks [Daniel 7:24; Rev 13:2 / Daniel 7:7]

4.) He will subdue three kings [Daniel 7:8, 24]

5.) He will confirm a covenant with "many", i.e. the Jewish people [Daniel 9:27]

6.) He will not answer to a higher earthly authority; "He will do as he pleases" [Daniel 11:36]

7.) He will show no regard for the religion of his ancestors [Daniel 11:37] nor for the desire of women.

8.) He will only honor a "god" of forces: the Economic/Religious Military Industrial Complex the CFR built. His whole focus and attention will be on his military. He will conquer lands and distribute them [Daniel 11:39-44]

He will rule over both an economic and a spiritual revival of the Greek/Roman Empire. The economic and spiritual part already exists and grows in power everyday via the CFR and its Dark Forces. But they have no one leader at present to command it all. That makes them ripe for the taking by the right person.

The 8th is interesting in that he will use both a socialists, conservative, and liberal method I pointed out early on the CFR uses to redistribute wealth. Only he goes a step further and uses the Military to achieve even more. The 7th fits more with a humanist ideology and the last part of it points to he will not be married. His attention will not be divided from his ultimate goal.

The 4th concerning his taking over from three Kings or rulers in the context of the Empires spoken on shows he comes on the political spotlight via a military and or political power grab where two of these Kingdoms will be part of the old Roman Empire. My thoughts on this based upon a hard look at these passages and on the world is Greece, Italy, and Spain. The economy of these three are perhaps the worst in the whole so called European Union. That makes them ripe for a power grab. But this also suggests he will not come out of either of those Nations. Egypt has had a revolution, but that revolution has tended to give more power to a group that does worship the God (Allah) of their fathers. That leaves Syria and Iran since we can discount ancient Babylon which tends itself to be Islamic more than secular. Syria at present has a rebellion going on and Iran has a growing split with it's secular leader and the youth. Also, the leader of Iran cannot stand

Israel enough to make any covenant with them. He's the one who wants to wipe Israel off the Planet. I think the place to suspect this leader to come from is Syria after their current leader falls unless Iran has a revolution and returns to its older ways that actually aided the Jews. Only, by the same passages I'd suggest this new friendship with Israel will be a way to take over there, not really help them.

What I am suggesting without any strong religious overtones is the World today is set up perfectly for just such a leader as the Anti-Christ to come into power. It would fulfill the power void that exists at the present with everything the CFR has set up and would be a fulfillment of their general goal of a one world government, or New World Order.

Is there anything else we can figure out?

His name as recorded in the Book of Revelations who's numerical value is 666 if you read the full context is not his birth name at all. It is a name he will take on after he comes to political power. Liken this to Alexander was not the Great until after he came to power. He had a regular family name prior to that. But Daniel does liken him to a Leopard. A Leopard has spots or different dark and light colors on its chest. One human trait that comes to mind is someone of mixed decent which would explain how he as an Arab could manage to befriend the Jews. It could also be he is of African and white decent along with Arab heritage. That being the case he can easily fit in with the lower European Nations, Israel, the Arabs, and Africans.

The He will not answer to a higher authority shows he will not follow America, Russia, or China's bidding. In fact, via control of the oil I suspect he will not be bothered by interference from any of these Nations who will probably welcome his peace efforts anyway. If one follows the rest with the 3.5 years of peace followed by 3.5 years leading to world War III. Here is where I suspect America, Russia, and China will move to take this leader on. China will move in across what today is Iran and Iraq headed North. The other forces will attack in the region of Lebanon which sits right between Israel and Syria which is another reason I suspect this leader will come of Syria. The rest of the World will attack his home base.

Why would America sit this one out? Same thing we did during the rise of Hitler was sit back. Russia at present befriends Syria and if Iran sides with this new Leader China has relations with them. A lot of this is itself in place due to work of the CFR.

Irrespective of your religious views you might be asking how all this could come about?

1.) We've let the Dark Forces of the CFR come about.

2.) We have never learned from the past.

Map of Modern Middle East

Map of Roman Empire

On September 23, 1947, right at the beginning of the "modern" UFO era, General Nathan Twining, Head of the U.S. Air Material Command (AMC), wrote a classified letter to Air Force General George Schulgen regarding the "flying discs." He said the objects were "real and not visionary or fictitious." They may possibly be natural phenomena, he wrote, such as meteors. But: the reported operating characteristics such as extreme rates of climb, maneuverability (particularly in roll), and action which must be considered evasive when sighted ... lend belief to the possibility that some of the objects are controlled either manually, automatically, or remotely. Twining listed several common descriptions of UFOs. They generally were silent, had a metallic or light reflecting surface, no trail, were circular or elliptical in shape, and often flat on the bottom. Many descriptions indicated a dome on top. Several reports indicated they flew in formation. Quite specific information, indeed.

On January 31, 1949, the FBI issued a memo on UFOs, entitled "Protection of Vital Installations." The classified document was sent to FBI Director J. Edgar Hoover, the Army's G-2, the Office of Naval Intelligence, and the Air Force Office of Special Investigations. It mentions a meeting among these groups concerning UFOs.
Here is a key statement of the document: "Army intelligence has recently said that "the matter of 'Unidentified Aircraft' or 'Unidentified Aerial Phenomena,' otherwise known as 'Flying Discs,' 'Flying Saucers,' and 'Balls of Fire,' is considered top secret by intelligence officers of both the Army and the Air Forces."

This is well after the time of Roswell and yet, all the while, government sources had been telling the public that this phenomenon was just a combination of hoaxes, hallucinations, conventional aircraft, and misidentification of natural phenomena. Why, then, was the subject considered top secret?

answer is contained within the memo itself. It mentions, for instance, a near-collision by an commercial airliner with a large "rocket" type craft (with windows, no less) traveling at an estimated speed of – strap yourself in – 2,700 mph. More serious, the memo explains, were invasions of sensitive airspace by unknown objects in the vicinity of the Atomic Energy Commission's installation at Los Alamos, New Mexico. The memo states that these had occurred throughout December 1948 (on the 5th, 6th, 7th, 8th, 11th, 13th, 14th, 20th, and 28th). The witnesses of these "unexplained phenomena" were "Special Agents of the Office of Special Investigation; Airline Pilots; Military Pilots, Los Alamos Security Inspectors, and private citizens." The sightings continued into 1949, as a similar object was seen in the area on January 6.
The memo goes on to explain that "recent observations have indicated that the unidentified phenomena travel at the rate of speed estimated at a minimum of three miles per second and a maximum of twelve miles per second, or a mean calculated speed of seven and one-half miles per second, or 27,000 miles per hour." Moreover, "on two separate occasions a definite vertical change in path was indicated." In other words, the phenomenon was able to maneuver at a very high rate of speed, and seemed to be focused on Los Alamos. The memo states that reports of the appearance of the object as typically round, occasionally diamond-shaped, "with a definite area to the light's source," and

having elongated trailing lights. "On two occasions reports have been received of the sighting of multiple units." There is some speculation within the document that the objects were Soviet in origin, but no evidence or proof is offered.

The memo also refers to "scientific reasons" why the objects could not be meteorites. "The only conclusions reached thus far are that they are either hitherto unobserved natural phenomena or that they are man made. No scientific experiments are known to exist in this country which could give rise to such phenomena." On the third page, the idea of "cosmic rays" was offered, though without any theory or evidence to support it.

On July 9, 1951, by the pilot of an F-51 fighter plane from Lawson Air Force Base in Georgia. The pilot, a combat veteran from World War Two, provided quite a bit of detail, which was recorded in the report.

"Object described as flat on top and bottom and appearing from a front view to have rounded edges and slightly beveled. From view as object dived from top of plane was completely round and spinning in clockwise direction.... Object did not appear to be aluminum. Only 1 object observed. Solar white. No vapor trails or exhaust or visible system of propulsion. Described as traveling [at] tremendous speed....Pilot states object was 300 to 400 feet from plane and appeared to be 10 to 15 feet in diameter....Pilot states he felt disturbance in the air described as 'bump' when object passed under plane....Pilot is considered by associates to be highly reliable, of mature judgment and a creditable observer."

H. Marshall Chadwell was the CIA's Director of Scientific Intelligence on December 2, 1942, and very much interested in this problem. In this memo, addressed to the CIA Director, General Walter Bedell Smith, Chadwell wrote:

"At this time, the reports of incidents convince us that there is something going on that must have immediate attention.... Sightings of unexplained objects at great altitudes and traveling at high speeds in the vicinity of major U.S. defense installations are of such nature that they are not attributable to natural phenomena or known types of aerial vehicles."

1954 at Maxwell, AFB

This report (headed "Emergency") originated from the flight service center at Maxwell Air Force Base, and was sent to the Commander of Air Defense Command (ADC) in Colorado.

The report describes the entry into airspace of a "strange stationary object variable in brilliance" which moved rapidly, then returned to its original position. The base sent a helicopter to investigate. The pilot's assessment: "definitely not a star." Many people watched this object from the tower, and a civilian tower radioed that it also had it in sight.

"...pilot of helicopter wished to stress fact that the object was of a saucer-like nature, was stationary at 2000 ft. And would be glad to be called upon to verify any statement and act as witness."

One of many classified reports that slipped through the cracks occurred at Minot Air Force Base, in North Dakota, on August 24, 1966. That night, an airman radioed to the base about a multicolored light, very high in the sky. A team went to the location, confirmed the original unknown, then saw a second, white object pass in front of clouds. The base radar tracked the object, which was as high as 100,000 feet (almost twenty miles). The object rose and descended several times; each time it descended, an air force officer in charge of a missile crew found his radio transmission interrupted by static, even though he was sixty feet below the ground. The object eventually descended to ground level ten to fifteen miles south of the area. The Air Force sent a strike team to check. Apparently, they saw the object either on the ground or hovering very low. According to the official report:

"When the team was about ten miles from the landing site, static disrupted radio contact with them. Five to eight minutes later, the glow diminished, and the UFO took off. Another UFO was visually sighted and confirmed by radar. The one that was first sighted passed beneath the second. Radar also confirmed this. The first made for altitude toward the north, and the second seemed to disappear with the glow of red."

Early in the morning on the March 16, 1967 at Malmstrom AFB in Montana, occurred one of the most extraordinary events in the history of military-UFO encounters. Under a clear and dark Montana sky, an airman with the Oscar Flight Launch Control Center (LCC) saw a star-like object zigzagging high above him. Soon, a larger and closer light also appeared, and acted in similar fashion. The airman called his NCO, and the two men watched the lights streak through the sky, maneuvering in impossible ways. The NCO phoned his commander, Lieutenant Robert Salas, who was below ground in the launch control center.

"Great," Salas said. "You just keep watching them and let me know if they get any closer."

A few minutes later, the NCO called again, shouting that a red, glowing UFO was hovering outside the front gate. "What do you want us to do?" asked the NCO. Salas told him to make sure the site was secure while he phoned the command post. "Sir," replied the NCO, "I have to go now, one of the guys just got injured."

Before Salas could ask about the injury, the NCO was off the line. The man, who was not seriously injured, was evacuated by helicopter to the base. Salas woke his commander, Lieutenant Fred Meiwald. As he briefed Meiwald, an alarm went off in the small capsule, and both men saw a "No-Go" light turn on for one of the missiles. Within seconds, several more missiles went down in succession.

Twenty miles away, at the Echo-Flight Launch Facilities, the same scenario was taking place. First Lieutenant Walter Figel, the Deputy Crew Commander of the Missile Combat Crew, was at his station when one of the Minuteman missiles went into "No-Go" status. He called the missile site and learned that a UFO had been hovering over the site. Like Salas, Figel doubted the story. But just then, ten more ICBMs in rapid succession reported a "No-Go" condition. Within seconds, the entire flight was down.

Strike teams were dispatched to two launch facilities, where maintenance crews were already at work. Figel had not told the strike teams about the UFO report. Upon their arrival, however, the teams reported back to him that all of the maintenance and security personnel had been watching UFOs hover over each of the sites.

The missiles were down for most of the day. Neither the Air Force investigation, nor the laboratory tests at Boeing's Seattle plant found any cause for the shutdown. According to the Boeing engineering chief, "there was no technical explanation that could explain the event." UFOs were not part of this analysis.

On the evening of October 31, 1975 at Wurtsmith AFB in Michigan, an airman saw what appeared to be running lights of a low flying craft, possibly a helicopter, near the southern perimeter of the base, heading westerly. One light pointed down; two red lights were near the back. The object was either silent or very quiet.

A little later, other witnesses saw several lights near the western edge of the base. The lights turned north and appeared to lose altitude. Most heard nothing, although some claimed to hear a quiet sound similar to a helicopter, but which faded quickly.
Then, three times within the space of 11 minutes, security police at the back gate reported that an object with no lights – possibly a helicopter – entered the base and hovered very low over the weapons storage area. Radar personnel detected low flying objects (plural) in the area. At the northern perimeter of the base, one of the crafts briefly turned its lights on.

A KC-135 tanker was flying to the base at the time. It was ordered to intercept and identify the object or objects. The crew tracked what at first appeared to be a single craft for about 35 miles southeast from the base. However, they soon decided they were seeing two objects, apparently communicating with each other with irregular flashing lights. Radar tracking's could not last longer than 10 seconds. Every time they tried to close, the objects simply pulled away.

The crew lost the objects among fishing boat lights in Saginaw Bay, so they started back. Here is how the story ends, as told by the navigator to the base historian four years later:

"On the way back, we picked the UFO up again at our eight o'clock position. We turned away, and it proceeded to follow us. Finally, we turned back in the direction of the UFO and it really took off back in the direction of the Bay area. I know this might sound crazy, but I would estimate that the UFO sped away from us doing approximately 1,000 knots. We continued in the direction of the Bay until RAPCON (radar) called us again and said they were painting a UFO four to five miles over the coast traveling in a westerly direction. They vectored us to the position of the UFO and we proceeded but at point we were low fuel and were forced to return to Wurtsmith. I remember that while on final approach we saw the lights again near the Weapons Storage Area. Following the mission we discussed the incident and about a week later, Captain Higgenbotham was questioned by OSI and cautioned not to discuss the incident."

On the night of September 18, 1976, the Iranian Air Force was involved in one of the most dramatic UFO events in modern history. Not only was the case itself extraordinary, but so was the documentation: namely, a four-page U.S. Defense Intelligence Agency report.

The strangeness began after 10:30 p.m. on September 18, when the control tower at Mehrabad Airport received calls about an unknown object hovering at 1,000 feet in the northern section of Teheran. The tower supervisor observed the object with binoculars, describing it as rectangular or cylindrical. In his words, "the two ends were pulsating with a whitish blue color. Around the mid-section was this small red light that kept going in a circle.... I was amazed."

He notified the Iranian Air Force. Two hundred miles away, at Shahrokhi AFB, General Nader Yousefi ordered an F-4 Phantom to investigate. It took off at 1:30 a.m. on the morning of September 19. According to the pilot, the object was intensely brilliant and "easily visible" at a distance of 70 miles. As he came to within 25 nautical miles (about 29 statute miles), his aircraft "lost all instrumentation and communications." He broke off the intercept and headed back, at which point his aircraft regained all instrumentation.

The General had already authorized a second F-4. When the second pilot reached a distance of 27 NM, he obtained a substantial radar return, "comparable to that of a 707 tanker." At this point, the UFO began to move away from the F-4 at the same speed. It was extremely bright and gave off flashing strobe lights arranged in a rectangular pattern. The colors alternated blue-green, red, and orange, although the sequence was so fast that they were almost simultaneous.

The UFO then released a bright object, "estimated to be one half to one third the apparent size of the Moon." It headed straight toward the F-4 "at a very fast rate of speed." The pilot tried to fire an AIM-9 missile at it, "but at that instant his weapons control panel went off and he lost all communications." Seeking to evade, he dove and turned away, but the object followed him and turned inside his own turn. It then returned to the main object "for a perfect rejoin." The F-4 pilot then regained communications and weapons control.

At this point, another object came out of the main object and rapidly descended. The F-4 crew observed this, anticipating an explosion. Instead, the object appeared to rest gently on the Earth and cast a very bright light over an area of about 2 miles. The crew noted the object's position and then headed back.

Before landing, they circled Mehrabad Airport several times, receiving frequent interference and losing communications. During their final approach, the F-4 crew saw a cylinder shaped object with bright steady lights on each end and a flasher in the middle. They inquired with the tower, which replied that there was no other known traffic in the area.

The next morning, the F-4 crew was taken in a helicopter to the area where the UFO was thought to have landed – a dry lake bed. They saw nothing, but picked up a beeper signal west of the area. At the point where the return was the loudest was a small house. They landed and asked the residents if they had noticed anything strange the previous night. The people mentioned a loud noise and a bright light, "like lightning."

In 2005, one of the Iranian pilots, General Parviz Jafari, confirmed the facts of the chase in an interview with Whitley Strieber and Dr. Roger Leir.

U.S. intelligence analysts found the case to be spectacular. An evaluation in the DIA files stated:

"An outstanding report. This case is a classic which meets all the criteria necessary for a valid study of the UFO phenomenon: a) the object was seen by multiple witnesses from different locations ... and viewpoints. b) the credibility of many of the witnesses was high (an Air Force general, qualified air crews, and experienced radar operators). c) visual sightings were confirmed by radar. d) similar electromagnetic effects (EME) were reported by three separate aircraft. e) there were physiological effects on some crew members (i.e. loss of night vision due to the brightness of the object). f) an inordinate amount of maneuverability was displayed by the UFOs."

My point in all this is that while it is true we lack at the public level a section of the crafts involved to put on display and study and we lack DNA evidence anyone who wants to say there is nothing to all these reports or that they are just Demons as some in the religious right say has a ton of circumstantial evidence it must overcome. In fact, more witnesses and circumstantial evidence than is required to get a convection in a trial. As for the Demon idea. First off these are physical craft able to be tracked on radar, viewed in many cases by highly trained people (Pilots,etc) reported as metallic and able to fly in ways nothing we have can. At least according to the Biblical definition of such as fallen angelic beings which are spiritual they would have no reason for real metallic crafts.

However, lets think outside the standard Christian Box for a moment. Let's go back to that verse describing the anti-Christ as worshipping a strange God of forces that his Father's never worshipped. The common description of Aliens, at least the one's the public tends to call Grays is rather reptilian in nature without the scales. Many times over the ancients in the Bible described Satan as a Great Dragon. Basically, a walking talking lizard. Let's suppose there is some truth in that. Let's just suppose instead of the standard idea on angels these are beings far more advanced than us. That not all of them visit us for good purposes. It is possible the "God of forces" and the "God his Father's never worshipped" is an Alien God. It would explain some of the miracle like powers mentioned in the Book of Revelations and the power the Beast displays. It could go a long way to answering how the Beast or Anti-Christ having been killed by a shot to the head is resurrected back to life and how a living breathing image or copy of him is created- The Image of the Beast- in Revelations. This being the case it is possible the one reason our Government or any other Government has never come forward and admitted what they know. Not much different from a science fiction story line behind the series V. If they can manipulate space-time I suspect they could alter other things to make themselves more fit the common Image of God many hold enough to fool most of the population into following after the Anti-Christ that serves them.

At the very least the amount of witnesses, the amount of documents, the amount of people over time that have seen these objects bears a more honest answer from our Government exactly what it is they have been lying about to the American public all these years and why. It's just another indication of the fact that our Government's elected officials cannot be trusted.

www.ingramcontent.com/pod-product-compliance
Lightning Source LLC
Chambersburg PA
CBHW041459280526
45792CB00004B/1061